Vitality
Therapy

# Vitality Therapy

## Techniques for Short-Term Counseling

*Dennis L. Gibson*

**BAKER BOOK HOUSE**
Grand Rapids, Michigan 49516

**Library of Congress Cataloging-in-Publication Data**

Gibson, Dennis L.
    Vitality therapy: techniques for short-term counseling /
    Dennis L. Gibson.

       p.     cm.
    Bibliography: p.
    ISBN 0-8010-3824-3
    1. Cognitive therapy.  2. Psychotherapy, Brief.  I. Title.
RC489.C63G53  1989                  89-6601
616.89'14—dc20                       CIP

To

**Bill Starr,**

who redirected my life
by his brief counsel
at the Midland-Bay City-Saginaw Airport:

"Denny, bash on through!"

and

To **Ruth Flesvig,**

my mother-in-law,
the briefest of counselors
with her trenchant maxim:

"Just do it!"

# Contents

Introduction     9

1 Encourage       15

2 Transfer        27

3 Reframe         37

4 Think the Unthinkable     75

5 Grieve     97

6 Use the Heart's Eye     107

7 Challenge Logic     129

8 Miscellaneous Tactics     145

9 A Verbatim Example     175

References     191

# Introduction

A young adult friend told me of his anxiety and frustration on a demanding new job at which he earnestly wanted to excel. He said that the level of responsibility to supervise other people overwhelmed him. I asked him what sentence he could think of that would most clearly express his frustration at the moments he felt it. What would capture the overwhelmed feeling in a nutshell? He thought a moment, then answered, "I look at all I'm supposed to do and think, 'It's too big for me.'"

That statement gave me an idea. I knew something about this young man and his interests. I had heard of his expertise in technical rock climbing, which required him to claw his way up sheer cliffs hundreds of feet high. I asked, "When you are out rock climbing, do you ever look up from the base of a cliff and say, 'That's too big for me'?" He instantly answered, "Never! I always know I can make any climb I attempt, just by putting out more energy at the tough places."

I next asked, "How can you apply the more-energy principle to the jobs that seem too big for you at work?" My friend paused a thoughtful couple of seconds, then mused, "The more-energy principle—it's really the same thing, isn't it? I mean I already have in me the attitude that I *can* handle hard rock climbs. Work is just another rock climb. I can use the more-energy principle there, too!"

Weeks later at our next contact, he reported to me that the phrase *more-energy principle* had repeatedly boosted his confidence when he faced some task he initially felt was too big for him. He said that he also calmed himself before stressful interviews by telling himself, "This is just another tough move on a rock climb."

THE CONCEPT. This example illustrates the basic tenet of any cognitive therapy approach. To put it in biblical terms, we are transformed by the renewing of our minds (Rom. 12:2). Clients often indicate mind-renewals by remarking after potent therapeutic interventions, "I never thought of it that way before." These comments inevitably accompany a release of creative energy within clients. They seem a bit more alive, hence the term *vitality therapy*. This book teaches techniques that arouse and unlock fragments of aliveness in a client. They initiate momentum in positive

directions quite opposite to the futile "stuckness" generally domi-
nating the attitudes of a troubled person.

Vitality-therapy techniques can equip even non-professional
counselors to accomplish small mind-renewals quickly. Many situations that part-time counselors face impose extreme time limita-
tions. An emergency telephone call to a crisis center may allow a
counselor only twenty minutes to make a strategic difference in a
caller's thinking. Similarly, physicians often hear weighty emotional problems from patients who mention them incidentally in
the midst of the doctor's tightly scheduled day. Of course, these
techniques can also enhance the effectiveness of a professional
counselor's work, which may involve a series of appointments over
weeks or months.

To address such a mixed audience of readers, this book sometimes refers to those who seek help as "people" and other times as
"clients." The counseling might be done in an office, a car, a restaurant, or a home, and in person or by phone.

Recent writings on "brief therapy" typically speak of five to ten
one-hour sessions, a week or two apart. But this book generally
holds to the premise that clients might not return after the first
meeting, so that counselors must make interventions as potent as
possible in their brief opportunities. This constraint rules out ex-
tensive diagnosis or history-taking and focuses instead on rapidly
relieving the distresses people bring to a session.

## A Perspective on Clients

When under emotional distress, most people are highly open to
influence. They are unsettled and looking for a new equilibrium.
Although they generally respond well to ordinary supportive as-
sistance from friends and counselors, some people resist such help
and frustrate their would-be helpers. I describe them in an earlier
book, *The Strong-Willed Adult* (1987).

Strong-willed adults have heavy doses of what psychologists call
obsessive-compulsive tendencies. When these persons come under
stress and seek help, they often maintain a virtual immunity to
common sense and ordinary appeals to reason. Why? Because in
their vulnerable state of arousal, they concentrate on protecting
themselves from losing face. They fight off simple solutions with

words like, "I already tried that." They discount obvious remedies because to solve a distressing problem quickly and easily would make them feel foolish for not having thought of it sooner.

Therefore, the counseling techniques that distinguish vitality therapy start off routinely enough to help ordinary sufferers. But they also aim at difficult clients who require novel methods to surprise and intrigue them out of self-defeating rigidity.

## A Perspective on Counseling

### Logjams

While counseling, I hold in my mind's eye a picture of myself as one of those lumber-company employees who walk out onto logs floating downriver toward the paper mill. I see myself carrying a long pole with which to push a key log or two that has caused the whole pack to jam and stop flowing downstream. Sometimes I find that just walking out onto the logs jostles them enough to free them. Usually, however, I have to nudge a particular log with my long pole to free it and point it downstream so that the rest can flow. Occasionally I need to dynamite a difficult jam.

Walking on the logs symbolizes my gentle listening, showing interest, and working to understand the problems that clients bring. Merely joining with people and working to understand their perspectives and experiences by restating them in my own words often liberates these people, be they my clients or my loved ones. Among strong-willed, obsessive clients, however, only a few unusually sociable ones find just the counselor's listening enough for them.

### Moving Key Logs

Poking at key logs with my long pole represents therapeutic techniques by which I raise uncertainty in clients' minds about faulty foundational beliefs that they have always taken for granted. I might call problematic behavior by a different name that casts it into a whole new light. For instance, reframing perfectionism as "thoroughness" sometimes frees clients to exclaim, "Well, I don't have to be *that* thorough."

I often exaggerate notions that clients mention, so that they chuckle at the caricature and take an oppressive thought less grimly than they used to. For example, a man refers to his perfectionistic wife as a "drill sergeant." I build playfully on his phrase as follows:

> "I can see it all now. White gloves. Parade-dress uniform. She barks out her commands. She court-martials the laggards. I mean this gal is on a power trip, right?"

The husband answers, "Well, she's not *that* bad."

Clients often come to counseling insisting that they cannot perform certain bold actions. I point out ways in which they are already doing the equivalent in another setting. For example, a shy young lady client complains that she cannot turn down sexual advances from men who date her. I point out that she already says *no* naturally and easily in other circumstances. For example, she readily refuses when I encourage her to do something in therapy, such as role-play raising her voice in an emphatic "No!" to an imaginary suitor.

### Blasting Big Jams

"Dynamite" corresponds to the intense, emotion-arousing confrontive techniques that I employ against particularly difficult resistances. These include imaging and role-play methods for healing painful memories. I might, for example, have a bereaved client sit in one chair and talk to an imaginary deceased loved one who is pictured as sitting in a second chair. If that loved one died before the client had a chance to say goodbye, I lead a tearful farewell scene in this two-chair format.

Another technique to get around resistances in a way that surprises clients is to use a devil's-advocate style. I may argue, for example, that a shouting couple ought to raise their voices still more, since they "have not yet managed to get through to each other." Some devoutly rebellious clients thus find themselves in a dilemma where they can continue rebelling only by *de*-creasing whatever they do that feeds their problems.

## Plan of This Book

Obviously the above progression moves from simple techniques, which minimally trained counselors can use in brief counseling, toward advanced techniques such as highly trained therapists would employ in long-term psychotherapy. Nevertheless, what this book presents ought to reach the middle 50 percent of people in distress. Of a hundred such, maybe the easiest twenty-five can find relief from thinking it through alone, or applying ideas from a self-help book, or talking informally with a loved one whose advice they welcome. The toughest twenty-five may require extended and intensive psychotherapy for many months—perhaps aided by medications, hospitalization, or a procedure such as electroshock therapy, all of which are essentially the province of medically trained psychiatrists.

Clients from that tough 25 percent give you the feeling that you are not doing enough for them. Easy clients focus largely "out there," on their difficult circumstances and what they can do about those. Tough clients turn the focus "in here," implying negative feelings toward you and your competence and caring. If two clients notice you stifling a yawn, the easy one will remark, "You must be tired," whereas the tough one will say, "I can tell you are fed up with me."

The clients in the middle 50 percent generally do not use "advice" per se, even if they ask for it. Therefore, their counselors must use a little more sophistication than a well-meaning friend or family member might. The techniques in vitality therapy offer some of that sophistication. They also supplement the training offered in most books for Christian lay counselors. These emphasize listening skills to convey attitudes of supportive warmth. This book starts there and goes on to more novel techniques for mind-renewal.

In general, chapters describe and illustrate several therapeutic techniques in an increasing order of complexity. Finally there is transcribed a typical counseling conversation, annotated with explanations of what technique the counselor is using and why.

# 1

# Encourage

Amy seats herself in my office for the first time. Before she can say a word, tears fill her eyes and she apologizes.

*Amy:* I wasn't going to cry.
*Counselor* [handing Amy a box of tissues]: Well, it looks like you need to.
*Amy:* [Laughs a little nervously, dabs her eyes, and says nothing for several seconds.]
*Counselor:* What's it about?
*Amy:* My husband told me he doesn't love me.
*Counselor:* Ouch! When was this? [Conveyed in a tone of "That news hurts me, too."]
*Amy:* Sunday night. Right out of the clear blue sky.
*Counselor:* So you had no inkling. It really caught you off guard.
*Amy:* [Nods and cries harder.]
*Counselor:* Well, no wonder you're feeling sad. I would, too, in your place.
*Amy:* [Continues crying.]
*Counselor:* And I'm impressed at how much you care about having a close relationship with your husband. Many women in your shoes take a bitter, hard attitude.

THE CONCEPT. In a dialogue like the above, I seek as a counselor to merge traffic with my client. I picture that I am jogging along some morning and see a friend ahead of me. I jog up to that friend and match stride so that we jog together. The process of counseling is often referred to as "coming alongside of." So, in the above dialogue, the counselor seeks to join Amy, to establish a rapport with her, to give the message "I am with you."

This joining operation consists of three categories of encouraging actions: showing interest, agreeing, and praising. Let's take a look at why these actions encourage a person like Amy.

First of all, every wounded person feels something like an outcast. Particularly in Amy's situation, her emotion comes from an experience of rejection by a loved one. She equates that with exclusion from the whole human race. And because her feelings are strong, she anticipates resistance from anyone else to whom she talks. Someone might say, "You shouldn't feel that way. Stop crying. Your tears make me uncomfortable." Or sometimes the negative response from the listener takes the form of condescension, such as, "There, there, honey. I'm here with you now and everything is going to be okay." Since that excessive reassurance implies the counselor's lack of confidence in Amy's coping capabilities, it quietly insults her.

By contrast, encouraging words convey respect. They reflect the counselor's belief that Amy's situation would certainly hurt *any* person. Furthermore, they affirm that her way of expressing her pain is perfectly understandable and beneficial. Encouragement lets her continue being the expert on her feelings. It does not imply that she is bad for being rejected, nor that she cannot work her way out of this temporarily paralyzing situation.

Counselors serve essentially as foster parents to those seeking help. Clients put themselves into a position of need and counselors into the role of providers. Throughout their lives, all persons add more and more links to a chain of parenting experiences, started early in life by the parent(s) who raised them. Therefore, present encounters call for counselors to do the three things that any good parents do for children: welcome, celebrate, and restrict. To put this in a simple way, all children need to hear from parents the words, "Hi!" and "Wow!" and "No!"

Considering "No!" first, *restriction* means setting limits on the misbehavior of persons who are out of control with hysterical emotion. Counselors introduce firm, reassuring structure by saying things like, "Hold it. Wait a minute. Slow down. Let's take things one at a time."

Our emphasis at this point, however, is on *encouragement*—the "Hi!" and "Wow!" Let's take a look now at three primary ways to "encourage."

## Show Interest

Showing interest in what a client says, by taking a position of eager listener, conveys a profound experience of respect and dignity to the speaker. The mere fact that you become quiet and attentive implies a positive message: "What you think and feel is worth my time and attention." Too often counselors speak of people being "worthwhile." They leave it as an unfinished concept, as if "worth" is something about the person, unrelated to anyone else *besides* that person. But "worth" is a value judgment that grows out of the opinion of an evaluating person. As listener, you give the speaker the experience of being worth *your* while. By your active interest, you cast the client into the role of an expert from whom you can learn something that you want to learn, namely that person's experience of one corner of life.

### Ask for Details

In the sample illustration dialogue with Amy, the counselor asks regarding Amy's tears: "What's it about?" This lays out a welcome mat for her, a red carpet to walk on into the conversation. Here is a list of other specific ways to ask for details:

"Tell me more."

"What prompted you to call?"

"What's going on with you?"

"What are you feeling?"

"Why don't you just tell me your whole story, and when I have a question about it, I will just interrupt and ask." (This expression of interest also conveys some structure, to help an over-anxious client know a little bit about how to function here in this unfamiliar setting.)

"What is all this doing to you emotionally?" (A good question to ask when the person obviously has feelings, but has not put them into words, hiding them instead behind a lot of description of events.)

Notice another encouraging element implied by this active grasping for details: it defines client and counselor as equals. The counselor who simply listens, like an inanimate tape recorder, shortchanges the client from the experience of a give-and-take relationship with another human being. However, when I as counselor interrupt as necessary in order to ask questions that allow me to understand the client, I convey an unspoken message:

We are partners together. I view you as having some valuable information to impart to me. I also consider you able to adapt to my handicap of having to have things said perhaps two or three times before I can grasp it. I certainly care too much about our relationship to let either of us fail to connect with the other.

### Say "Mhmm" "Wow!" and "Ow!"

These unobtrusive brief responses do wonders to keep the client's expression of thoughts and feeling flowing. They lubricate the communication process. They impart the unspoken message that I am with you and not interrupting you at this time. In particular, the simple *mhmm* type of response goes with a head nod. These are the usual nonverbal signals that listeners use to give speakers a green light to continue in the direction they are going. Without adequate signals of this kind, insecure speakers often interrupt their train of thought in order to ask, "Are you following me? Do you know what I mean?"

Now about when and how to say "Wow!" A seven-year-old girl, riding a bicycle in front of her house and successfully keeping her balance for the first time, cries out proudly, "Look, Mommy, I'm doing it!" Any good mother celebrates the moment with some version of "Wow!"

Clients occasionally brag timidly when indeed they should brag heartily. Amy, the client in the illustration opening this chapter, might say something like this: "My husband may not love me, and I may feel heartbroken, but I am determined to give this marriage my best shot." The counselor could validate such a spunky stance with some words like these:

"Good for you!"

"That'a girl!"

"I *like* that!"

"Well said!"

"Nice going!"

"You bet!"

"Dynamite!"

"Super!"

"I'm proud of you!"

Saying "Ow!" goes a step beyond empathy into sympathy. Many

manuals on counseling skills emphasize empathy and distinguish it from sympathy. Counselors often go too far and eliminate sympathy from their way of participating with a client. This artificially stiffens and sterilizes the relationship. Of course, it is easy to make a mistake at the extreme of being *too* sympathetic, thus imparting a maudlin message of "You poor baby. You fragile thing!"

Balanced sympathy normalizes clients' painful experiences as something common to mankind and an appropriate expression of the pain that anyone in their circumstances would feel. This balance comes across best by brevity. Tone of voice and the look on the counselor's countenance communicates 90 percent of the caring message: "I'm sorry to hear that," or "That's no fun."

### Say It Back

In the dialogue with Amy at the start of this chapter, she tells of her husband's announcement that he no longer loves her. As counselor I ask when this happened, and Amy answers, "Sunday night. Right out of the clear blue sky." I then say back to Amy her basic message in *my* words: "So you had no inkling. It really caught you off guard."

The main counseling technique used in most lay-counselor training is active listening. It is the primary skill that Dr. Thomas Gordon teaches parents to use in his book (*Parent Effectiveness Training* [1970]) and in his courses by the same name. It goes beyond merely hearing, accepting, and digesting what clients say. It includes the next step of working with clients to be sure that I, the counselor, have accurately taken in and understood what they meant to get across to me.

This basic human-relations skill also nourishes my good relationship with my wife, particularly when she tries to communicate to me some distress that she has a hard time clarifying for herself. In my role as listener to her, it often helps me to picture myself as an obstetrician in a delivery room, helping my wife to give birth to her baby ideas and feelings. I want to draw them forth. I want to protect their fragile vitality, expressed in her initial trial formulations of what she thinks and feels at the moment.

I take great care to neither scoff nor make any evaluative comments on what she says until she has strengthened her own verbalization of the thought or feeling to the point where she can say quite solidly, "Yes, this *is* what I'm really thinking and feeling." I help her come to that solidity by my willingness to serve her as a sounding board. She can try her thoughts on me, for me to say them back to her in my words but without intruding any of my ideas. When she hears her own thoughts and feelings come back, it helps her think further—"Is that what I really mean?"

The following list offers words and phrases that help me as a listener to maintain a frame of mind of wanting to digest what the speaker says:

"Let me see if I am reading you right."

"In other words. . . ."

"What I hear you saying is. . . ."

"Would I be on track with you if I said it this way. . . ?"

### *Slow It Down*

In this aspect of active listening, I sometimes playfully take an attitude that I refer to as that of an "educable retardate." I comment to the speaker, "I am not quite sure I've got straight what you are saying. Could you please say it to me again in a little different way? I am a slow learner, but if you will work with me patiently and persistently enough, I will finally get the drift and then be with you in your message."

This attitude comes across as nonthreatening, as compared to its opposite, in which the listener pontificates as a know-it-all, with statements like, "Well, what you really mean is. . . ." Or sometimes amateur listeners speak as if they were psychological experts, saying things like, "The only reason you're saying this is because you're actually angry behind your tears." Such statements discredit what the speaker says. They put barriers in the way of the speaker's thinking process and impede the relationship between speaker and listener.

Speakers also benefit from their listeners' "slow learning." By having to restate their own message two or three different ways, speakers come to hear themselves and review their own thinking to the point where they sometimes modify it. When speakers have to teach someone else about their own perspective, they typically find inconsistencies, distortions, and things that on second thought they don't really mean. Good listeners thus provide a mental scratch pad for speakers, showing mercy by not holding speakers responsible for rough-draft versions of their thinking.

### Suspend Evaluations

When actively listening, do not add ideas of your own, including your agreement (or disagreement) with what the speaker says. Especially when clarifying their feelings, speakers often need the freedom to exaggerate. In order to zero in on an accurate expression of what they feel, they probably need to overshoot and undershoot. They will generally correct themselves without your help, for example, when they overstate their anger by saying things like, "I hate his guts. I never want to see him again! I don't care if he lives or dies!" Rather than say, "You don't really mean that," simply summarize what the speaker has said with words like, "You are so fed up that you're through."

Particularly when you counsel well-educated persons, you serve them as a sounding board because you join with the way they already think. Such people typically solve problems on their own by talking to themselves, perhaps even carrying on internal debates. You help them to hear themselves better when you give them a live audience off whom they can bounce their embryonic thoughts.

### Show Some Astonishment

Sometimes listeners can go a cautious step beyond mere active listening. When done in a strictly technical manner, participatory listening puts listeners into the position of living tape recorders, simply enabling speakers to play back their own thoughts and feelings. But listeners can also broadcast back to speakers a little bit of response, revealing how the speakers have affected them as listeners and thus how they probably affect other persons in their orbit.

For example, a wounded wife says of her husband, "I never want anything to do with him again!" Now if she is just expressing the first heat of her strong outrage, you would respond passively with *mhmm* or with active listening: "You're fed up with him. You've had it." If she is only blowing off steam, these responses help her to de-escalate. However, if she has passed that initial point and is now expressing a more entrenched bitterness, you might inch a step further with a challenge like this: "Never?" You use a tone of voice that is a little incredulous. Or, if you prefer a longer sentence, you could ask in an amazed tone of voice, "You *never* want *anything* to do with him *ever* again?"

You hope, of course, with these expressions of mild astonishment, to bring out what you sense *behind* the woman's hurt— a strong attachment to her husband and thus her imminent move from anger to sadness. You want to trigger her into that appropriate mourning phase, which she is stalling off by staying in anger. In other cases, with clients not so emotional, who are simply thinking through a topic on which they have conflicting thoughts, your mild amazement can promote insights on their part. After all, in the process of using a mental scratch pad, the speaker's thoughts are in quite malleable form.

Be careful when using this technique. Since it calls for you to mildly disagree with people, you run the risk of becoming an opponent who they feel has betrayed them. You can probably not use this tactic until you have built some capital in your emotional bank account with a client by the other means of rapport that are described here. You might want to cushion this intervention with a little playfulness, shown by a twinkle in your eye or a little nonverbal clowning. But you cannot get by with this kind of thing until you have made friends. So, before you can disagree, you have to build a wealth of trustworthiness.

Let's turn now to how you can accumulate some of that money in the bank by the technique of agreeing.

## Agree

In the illustrative dialogue with Amy at the start of this chapter, the counselor agrees with Amy when she cries and he says, "Well, no wonder you're feeling sad. I would, too, in your place." Note that the counselor comes alongside Amy but does not take sides. In other words, he agrees that she certainly has a perfect right to feel sad and tearful in her situation as she sees it. But the counselor does not formulate any kind of judgment against the husband for the wrongdoing that Amy has reported. The counselor does not yet know if Amy understood the husband correctly, or if the husband may have changed his mind since he said what hurt Amy. The counselor therefore suspends judgment on that, not embittering Amy by comments like, "What a louse your husband is."

The agreeing by which a counselor builds rapport with clients involves legitimatizing their feelings. It reassures clients that they still hold membership in the human race, without saying so in such a direct way that they wonder if perhaps their status was up for grabs. Here follows a list of agreeing statements that you might make in response to strong emotional expressions from clients:

"I don't blame you."

"That *is* rough."

"You really have been through the mill."

"What a heartbreak!"

"How frustrating!"

"That's terrifying!"

"Sure!"

"I'll bet!"

"Go right ahead and cry."

Please note that I do not include a statement like, "I know exactly how you feel." Avoid that like the plague! You do *not* know exactly how others feel. You are trying very hard to detect and understand and approximate a grasp of how your clients feel. But their feelings in a particular situation are like snowflakes—unrepeatable, different from anyone else's particular experience.

You may know somewhat how a client feels, based on similar experiences you have had, and it probably will help in your rapport with that person if you later indicate that you have gone through a similar situation. But always describe your experience as being different and probably not as difficult as the client's. You must avoid any kind of superior mine-is-worse-than-yours attitude. That minimizes the significance of what the other person experienced, just as surely as if you said, "You think that's bad? That's nothing compared to what *I've* been through."

Sometimes mental pictures help me to achieve a proper way of functioning with clients. For example, when coming alongside them by agreeing, I see myself standing next to them, singing a duet. I try to harmonize with the notes that they sing so that we make music together and share an experience.

## Praise

At the end of the dialogue with Amy, the counselor says, "And I'm impressed at how much you care about having a close relationship with your husband. Many women in your shoes take a bitter, hard attitude." The counselor here goes beyond agreeing with Amy's right to feel as she does, and in fact points out an additional positive factor that Amy herself did not mention. The counselor at this point takes this attitude: "I see something about you that you may not even realize, but that I like."

Clients resemble desert flowers, just ready to blossom upon the first rain shower of affirmation. They soak it up—and beam. Sometimes you know the moment you say the words that you have just made a friend for life. Clients' muscles visibly relax and they settle into their chairs. Praising is one of the most significant, impactful, positive things you can do. It goes back to the concept of foster-parenting, the "Wow!" aspect, celebrating the clients' capability and likeability.

### Don't Flatter

I distinguish between praise and flattery. Praise nourishes a person's dignity; flattery feeds his or her vanity. Flattery grows out of my own selfish motivation to get people to like me or make life easier for me. It is bribery with words. Notice the difference between the two in these examples:

*Flattery:* "You're such a terrific person that I'm sure you won't have any trouble at all adjusting to your new situation."

*Praise:* "It probably won't be easy, but I think you have shown qualities of fortitude in the past that will serve you well in the situation you now face."

*Flattery:* "You're the most courageous person I have ever met."

*Praise:* "I'm impressed at the courage you have shown in doing the right thing even when it wasn't easy."

*Flattery:* "You're the greatest."

*Praise:* "I like the way you do that."

There are several things that can genuinely impress me as a counselor within a few minutes of talking with people. For example, I can construe as a virtue even the very anguish with which they describe their situation. It implies earnestness, willingness to invest effort, a sober assessment of their situations, instead of an escapist attitude.

Near the end of a counseling conversation, compliments serve a valuable function of summarizing and bringing closure. At this point I might say, "Well, you have certainly expressed yourself forthrightly here." I would especially offer that to clients who have bawled me out. It's a soft answer that turns away wrath. Particularly at the end of an extended counseling conversation, people develop a kind of closure hunger. They need some way to wrap up, to believe that they have accomplished something, and to feel a sense of hope about their future direction. Compliments provide that because they have a kind of "goodbye" feature to them. They also signify what clients have going for them in positive directions.

### Share First Impressions

Sometimes I point out strong positive character traits in clients that are based on my first impressions of them. People especially appreciate this since they seldom learn how they affect others. The usual social conventions keep strangers from that kind of candid exchange.

For example, I might say to a person who has discussed feelings of shyness:

> You have talked with me today about your shyness, and I'm sure that you feel it in a painful way. But, in a way, I have to say I'm surprised. I don't think you see yourself like other people see you. The very first time we greeted each other out in the waiting room, you instantly made eye contact with me, stretched your hand out to shake mine, and introduced yourself. You immediately put me at ease. I would call that a healthy boldness.

In that example, I give concrete evidence of what I see as a positive character trait in the person. I do not say vaguely, "You're not as bad as you think you are." I cite specific behavior of the person and its positive impact on me.

When I lack specific evidence, I share with the person a kind of hunch or feeling I have. For example, a junior-high girl calls on the phone and says she is heartbroken because she just lost her best friend. I have a successful phone conversation that defuses the problem and sets her back into an optimistic frame of mind. Then, to wind up on an encouraging note, I might say:

> Something tells me that you're not going to have a very hard time in replacing this friend you just lost or other ones you're likely to lose in the future since that's the way life goes. You have expressed some

deeply human qualities here to me in our conversation, and my hunch is that I am not the only person who sees that side of you.

I am careful in my compliments not to obligate clients, since that gets back to flattery. By their unrealistic praise, parents often obligate their children to perform outstandingly: "You get back in that race and try again. You're the best kid out on the track today. You're going to win this race, and don't you tell yourself otherwise."

Youngsters who hear this kind of pep talk go away with the feeling that they will tragically disappoint their parents if they don't deliver a superhuman performance. Better that the parent say something like, "I am eager to see you run this race. Give it your best and then let's talk later about how it felt."

When you take this orientation as a parent, the child does not have to *win* in order to please you but just compete. You will be disappointed if the young person does not *strive,* but the level of achievement matters far less to you than the fact of his or her participation.

Be careful to cast a vote of confidence instead of telling people that their problems will go away. Give this message: "Even if this situation doesn't work out the way you hope it will, I'm sure that you have what it takes to learn from the experience and be a better person because of it." That is much better than telling people that "things will not be as bad as you fear. Mark my words. Just wait and see."

You can also formulate genuine compliments from whatever level of health the person already shows. Going back to the illustration with Amy, the counselor mentioned that many other women in her shoes take a bitter, hard attitude toward husbands who stop loving them. The fact that Amy does *not* take a bitter attitude implies strength in her. In other words, something good is already going on within Amy that makes her a healthier person than she might be, considering the circumstances. Here again, a little bit of astonishment can help boost the person. You might say, "I'm surprised you're not feeling far worse than you are. What do you have going for you that keeps you from being absolutely paralyzed in this situation?"

This technique of surveying what clients already have going for them forms the basis for the next chapter. Your encouragement can help them discover that they have tools in one area of competent living that can serve them well in the problem area. All they have to do is "transfer."

# 2

# Transfer

THE CONCEPT. The story that opens the introduction of this book illustrates the use of the "transfer" technique. The young rock-climber *transferred* a problem-solving skill from the recreational area of his life into the vocational area. As counselor I merely asked questions that helped him to access a solution he already had but simply did not know he had when he faced a new problem.

Most people seeking help have already solved, in some other department of their lives, a problem similar to the one now plaguing them. They simply have not thought of transferring that old solution to this new problem. I often picture their lives as a jigsaw puzzle if I know they have a piece somewhere to fit the hole they tell me about. Generally, *I* can recognize those key puzzle pieces better than my clients can, simply because they are too close to their own situations to see them in perspective—the old forest-and-trees dilemma.

When people call me for an appointment, it is usually one of several steps they are taking in the direction of making things better. Setting an appointment in itself reflects some optimism for the future. I seek to discover the momentum they already have in the direction of improvement, then merge with it and enhance it. In other words, they are already doing something that I want them to do more of.

All people and relationships show irregular patterns of strengths and weaknesses. I keep two questions in the back of my mind to guide myself in working with people and to occasionally ask them: (1) "Why aren't you worse?" and (2) "What keeps you from applying *that* skill to *this* problem?"

## "Why Aren't You Worse?"

### Burdened Clients

After clients have unloaded a list of burdens, you can commiserate therapeutically something like this: "Whew! With all that weighing you down, how do you manage at all?" Most clients will respond with a statement like, "Sometimes I wonder," and then go on to cite some things that bolster them. A man may mention how supportive his wife is. A woman may say that her family always had the motto "Never say die!" Someone else may reflect, "I guess I just keep telling myself that things are *so* bad, they can only get better."

Just facing your question often prompts clients to take an informal inventory of their coping skills. They claim conscious ownership of something positive already at work in their lives. When they put it into words, they settle into some variation of a hope-inducing notion: "Hey, I can count on that even more than I have been."

### Depressed Clients

Suppose a depressed woman comes to you for counseling. She describes herself as having no interest in anything—no pleasures, no motivation. But you notice that she dresses immaculately. So you ask, "How do you manage to keep yourself so well groomed? With your motivation all gone, how come you're not dirty and sloppy in your appearance?"

She answers, "That's a given. I mean, I'm simply not going to let myself go to pot, no matter what. That's one place where I draw the line."

You then raise the question of how many other "givens" she might consider including behind "the line" she draws. You build on the strength you find in her non-negotiable, no-matter-what resolve regarding her grooming. You ask if she would be willing to add one small anti-depressive action to her daily routine, as if it were an essential article of clothing. For example, you might propose that she call one elderly shut-in per day, just to cheer that senior citizen with a five-minute phone call.

Small considerate actions toward other people, of course, break the grip of self-centeredness with which depression strangles its sufferers. However, if you merely prescribed such actions to the depressed woman above, she probably would not find the motivation or energy to do them, even though she might agree that she would feel better if she did. So, finding how she motivates herself to do something she *does* do becomes the key to getting her to add the new action that will benefit her.

### Suicidal Clients

I routinely ask suicidally depressed clients in my first meeting if they will consider making a permanent decision never to take their own lives, "no matter what." Such people frequently answer, "Oh, I would never kill myself." That then gives me an opportunity to explore with them how they have decided to continue living whereas other people in similar depressing circumstances have given up and killed themselves. As they answer that question, they can't help but review their lives and skills.

Chapter 8 in this book ("Miscellaneous Tactics") tells when and how to ask the no-suicide question. It is one of the most health-creating interventions in vitality therapy since it penetrates to the bedrock of vitality—the zest for life.

## "You're Already Doing It"

### On the Job

A woman approached me after I had spoken to a group of single parents. She said she felt like a stranger to her teenage son. I asked what kind of work she did. After she said she sold real estate, I pointed out that on the job she got to know strangers quickly and skillfully every day. Then I asked, "Is there anything to keep you from using with the stranger at home the same skills you use with strangers at work?"

Her face lit up. She remarked that the key in establishing rapport with customers was to find out about their interests. She realized she knew how to do that—she could draw people out. Then she concluded, "So, I'm already good at doing what I need to do with my son."

### Within Problems

The problems that clients present can in themselves offer gold mines of strengths to marshal for problem solving. Many symptoms contain the seeds of their own cure. For example, addictions, like any other obsessions or compulsions, represent the ability to strongly devote oneself to the object of desire. Hence the success of such spiritually based treatment programs as Alcoholics Anonymous, which calls for devotion to a new object—sobriety.

It may sound strange to think of bad habits as having any redeeming features. But think about it—nothing characterizes a bad habit more than persistence! And persistence is precisely that character trait needed by someone who has begun using a workable procedure to solve a problem and merely stopped using it too soon.

Examples of the need for persistence typically come up when a counselor tries to help married couples change their patterns of communication. A wife complains that her husband never compliments her. The husband counterattacks by maintaining that nothing he ever tells her is enough to satisfy her. A counselor might prematurely urge the husband, nevertheless, to give the wife a compliment right there on the spot in the office. The husband turns to his wife and says, "I think you're a good cook." The wife rejects this compliment by saying, "You could just as easily have a maid prepare the meals for you, for all you care." She is bitter and discouraged and she shows it by not letting her guard down at the husband's first invitation. The husband turns to the counselor and says with a shrug of despair, "See, what did I tell you? It doesn't do any good to compliment her."

Rather than just urging this husband to begin complimenting his wife, as counselor I would prepare the husband for the wife's probable rejections. In other words, I would teach the husband "persistence" as part of the whole process of changing the balance of their communication from complaints to affirmations. I might even predict to the husband, in the wife's presence, that the wife will throw away at least the first four compliments that the husband gives her.

I would label these rejections on the wife's part as *positive:* she is not gullible but instead tests to see when the husband really does turn over a new leaf. She doesn't just want him to cheaply and easily win her trust. I may even tell this husband that he was wise to marry a woman who is no fool. After all, he would not want his wife falling for just anybody's line of praise, would he? Then she would be a sucker for every smooth-talking guy who came along. I point out that his wife is showing us here in the office that she really checks out the sincerity of people who praise her, by seeing their willingness to persevere. For clients familiar with Bible passages, I would remind them of the advice in James 1:3 to consider it a joy and a privilege whenever we face trials of different kinds, because trials enable us to develop perseverance—a valuable, godly character trait.

In this example I help the husband to view the wife's initial refusal of his compliments in a whole new light. I have relabeled it, changing its perception as evidence of futility into a demonstration of integrity on her part and opportunity for growth on his part. At the same time, I have created a tender trap for the wife. If she fulfills my prediction by throwing away her husband's first four compliments, her behavior now represents an act of cooperation with marriage counseling, rather than opposition to it.

As a paradoxical technique, I might even encourage this wife to refuse at least the first four compliments as a way of *helping her husband* practice the valuable, manly skill of perseverance. If she defies my prescription and disproves my predictions by accepting her husband's first compliment, so much the better! Then she will be working with him by reinforcing his thoughtful actions.

## "We Did It Before, and We Can Do It Again"

Those inspiring words helped fuel the energy of patriotism in the early 1940s as the United States geared up to fight in World War II. What a terrifying, deadly, costly ordeal lay before the nation! How could we possibly handle such a horrifying task? Answer: just like we did *before,* when we fought and succeeded in World War I.

### Childhood Achievements

Every needy person you ever try to help has already completed some equivalent of World War I. People with perfectionistic tendencies often speak about the horrible possibility that they might make a mistake. They hold back from active, creative, adventuresome activities on the basis that they might mess up and look foolish. You can point out to them that they have already come through the most intense period of trial-and-error learning in their lives: learning to walk and talk.

In learning to walk, I point out, they frequently fell down and even injured themselves. But they got up and went on again because the goal of walking so absorbed them. And the freedom of movement that it opened up for them made the price of frustration, humiliation, and injury well worth it. Learning to talk required even more practice and failure. They mispronounced words and misused phrases over and over again. And critics relentlessly corrected their errors.

People often discredit that example by saying, "But I didn't know any better then." I respond by saying that I'm not sure that what they know now really *is* better, because if they had made as big a deal of "failure" in toddlerhood as they do now, they would have given up on learning how to walk and talk.

### The School of Hard Knocks

Fear and discouragement typify over half the problems that people bring to you. When they tell you about the overwhelming situation they face, you can sometimes ask them to tell you about another occasion earlier in their lives when a similar "unbearable" difficulty occurred. Then ask how they handled it. Some persons will tell you, "I *didn't* handle it!" But you can tell them that they obviously did handle it one way or another, or else they would not be here to carry on a conversation with you at the moment. Often they will persist in arguing for the "impossibility" of managing their current hardship, by criticizing how they handled the earlier one. Redirect that answer toward further thinking by asking, "If you could live that situation over again, what would you do differently this time?"

Your questions can turn their thinking toward dealing with problems instead of halting before them. In discouragement, people repeatedly rehearse the impossibilities of their situation. You loosen up this gloomy process by merely increasing the proportion of their time that they talk about possibilities and a satisfactory future.

### A Biblical Example

Some quick-thinking counselors demonstrated a principle 2,700 years ago that we can use today with persons who resist sound advice out of misplaced pride. These wise men argued from the greater achievement to the lesser, a variation on "We did it before, and we can do it again."

Naaman, a high-ranking Syrian military commander, traveled to Israel so the prophet Elisha would cure his leprosy. Like a typical strong-willed adult, Naaman went off in a rage when Elisha did not heal him in the manner he expected and preferred. He objected, saying, "I thought that he would surely come out to me and stand and call on the name of the LORD his God, wave his hand over the spot and cure me of my leprosy" (2 Kings 5:11).

Elisha instead had sent a messenger to tell Naaman to wash himself seven times in the Jordan River. That was the wrong way, according to Naaman. He sounded like children who object when Daddy puts them to bed by a different ritual then Mommy uses— covers pulled up to the chin, then a kiss on the left side of the forehead not the right, then the teddy bear tucked in on the right not the left, and so on.

Note the pithy intervention by which Naaman's servants persuaded him not to leave Israel with his leprosy uncured: "My father, if the prophet had told you to do some great thing, would you not have done it? How much more then, when he tells you, 'Wash and be cleansed'!" (2 Kings 5:13).

At this logic Naaman did wash in the Jordan and was cleansed. When he saw the situation differently, his emotion changed and he became free to take the action he could not take earlier.

### Sometimes Less Is Better

Clients often prefer monumental suffering over simple, direct action. For example, parents of a child with school phobia might willingly pay hundreds of dollars for months of testing and therapy. Often, though, they can resolve the problem simply by making the child go to school. If you prescribe such an uncomplicated solution, the parents might object, "Oh, we could never do that." You could then observe to them that they are devoted parents who would readily take big and costly steps of therapy if it would help their daughter. How much more then would they not screw up their courage, set a firm rule that the child must go to school, then consistently enforce it in spite of the heartrending excuses the girl may try for two or three days!

Regarding school-phobic children, let me caution that in five or ten percent of the cases, they have legitimate reasons to fear going to school. For example, bullies may have been beating them up. Or teachers may have singled them out for unkind ridicule. Wise parents give kids a chance to report such difficulties. Parents ought not to say, "I don't want to hear *why* you don't want to go to school. You're going, period!" Parents instead should offer children the chance to explain.

With kids who merely whine, "I just don't want to. I'm afraid. I don't like it. I might get sick," parents must take a firm stand: "If there is ever any harmful situation at school that you need help to handle, I want to know about it so that you can go safely. But simply not liking school, or being generally afraid of it, is not reason enough to stay home. You *must* go."

That "must" means the parent is willing to physically drag to school a child who does not want to go voluntarily! And when a child stays home sick, that means *in bed*—no TV, no fun—a boring ordeal compared to school.

## "I Can See It All Now"

Let us return to the idea of getting a troubled person to antici-pate an untroubled future. Simply describing some petty details of what they *might* be doing in that future scene often gives people ideas that they can begin putting into effect now to help make that future a reality.

Suppose XYZ represents remedial action that a person resists doing. To get the person thinking about doing XYZ, I ask questions like these:

"What would you like most about doing XYZ if you could?"

"What would you like least?"

"What would be the easiest part about doing it?"

"If you suddenly woke up from sleepwalking or something, and found yourself doing XYZ, how would you know you were doing it?"

"Who else would notice?"

"How would they know that you were doing XYZ?"

"If you were going to demonstrate to some other people what you mean by 'doing XYZ,' how would you begin?"

"What would you show them next?"

"How would you probably help them if they were having trouble learning to do XYZ?" (Sometimes people can supervise some-one else in solving a problem that they do not consider them-selves able to solve. Their helpfulness gets them over their paralysis.)

These questions, asked one at a time, give clients repeated op-portunities to think of themselves as successfully performing the

XYZ action that they don't think they can do. Whether it be a depressed man returning to work, an alienated wife rekindling feelings of love toward her husband, a phobic person taking an airplane trip, or a perfectionistic student submitting a term paper containing two known typographical errors, in each case any question I ask them about a future that contains their completion of XYZ gets them rehearsing it more and more as a congenial possibility. I thereby unobtrusively get them to entertain a notion that they would fight off if I told them directly, "Pretend you are doing XYZ."

My curious questions change the apparent purpose of the conversation in the client's mind. No longer is it: "This counselor is trying to make me change." Instead, it is: "I am doing this counselor a favor by helping to satisfy his curiosity."

I might also ask for a picture of the future in the following way:

> Suppose that some months from now you and I were to meet and I would show you two one-minute video clips of yourself. One would come from yesterday, when your problem was bothering you. The other one would come from a time in the future after you have solved your problem. If nobody told you which was which, how would you know which one was 'before' and which one was 'after'?

This chapter has described ways of borrowing solutions to present problems from either past experiences or future possibilities. These techniques help clients to see their problems in a new way, not as unprecedented obstacles, but as minor variations on familiar tasks.

Seeing with new eyes becomes even more the goal of the techniques in the next chapter, on how to "reframe."

# 3

# Reframe

I sat at a telephone counseling service. The phone rang. A man sobbing on the other end told me that his wife was living with another man. She would call her husband every day, saying that she loved both men and just couldn't make her mind up which way to go. This Christian husband said that every time he thought about it he felt pain that he could hardly bear. He told me that he had prayed to God over and over again to remove the pain. Christian friends had also prayed over him and laid hands on him, asking that God would remove the pain and bring the wife back.

After talking with him for several minutes, I asked him where in his body he felt the pain. He said, "In my heart." I told him I had an idea that might sound a little crazy to him, but it seemed to me there might be some value in the pain that God allowed him to experience in his heart. The time of our conversation was shortly before Good Friday that year, and I knew that this caller was a devout Roman Catholic who observed Lent scrupulously.

I said that every time he felt that stab of pain in his heart, he was experiencing something of what Jesus experienced on the cross when he cried out, "My God, my God, why have you forsaken me?"

The man burst into tears, saying, "Yes! Yes! That's true! That's it!" His tears blended sorrow, appreciation, holy reverence, and relief. I went on to say, "Probably the greatest pain that Jesus experienced on the cross came not from the nails, but the sword of sorrow that stabbed into his heart. The crucifixion story will always in the future have a deeper meaning to you than ever before, because you are experiencing during this time of hardship in your life something of the sufferings of Jesus on the cross. That helps you to know him better and to join in the fellowship of his sufferings." I asked my caller if he was familiar with the quotation from Scripture to which my words referred. He said he was not, so I read it to him: "I want to know Christ and the power of his resurrection and the fellowship of sharing in his sufferings, becoming like him in his death" [Phil. 3:10]. More tears.

I went on to pray with this man that his wife would return to her wedding vows. I prayed that she would become disillusioned with her other lover and even physically nauseated when in his presence. I urged the husband not to divorce his wife. I said that perhaps God might

restore his wife to him and relieve him of anxiety and give him great joy
in rebuilding a godly marriage. But meanwhile every time that heartache comes, instead of trying to send it away, he should welcome it as an
opportunity to experience in his own body and emotions a little bit more
of what his Savior experienced, and thereby grow more fully equipped
than ever before as a soldier of Christ.

The man ended our twenty-minute phone conversation by saying he
felt much better and that he had never thought of his sufferings in that
way before, but it made a great deal of sense to him. He went on his way
rejoicing.

THE CONCEPT. The main healing ingredient in the above conversation came from the renewing of the man's mind by the switch
in meaning that I attached to his sufferings. Instead of its being
merely an ordeal that was unjust, painful, and meaningless, I referred to it as "an opportunity." That opened for this man an orientation that was very strong in him—to be a diligent student of the
things of Christ. He came to see that he could turn his marital
difficulties into spiritual learning experiences. This gave him hope
to carry him through the pain. In his profound book on suffering,
*Man's Search for Meaning,* Dr. Viktor Frankl quotes Nietzsche,
"He who has a *why* to live can bear with almost any *how*" (Frankl
1963, xi).

## Labels as Choices

Shakespeare said, "That which we call a rose/By any other name
would smell as sweet." Every item, event, and experience in our
lives can be called or described or labeled in many different ways.
The particular label we select depends on the purpose we have in
mind and determines the feelings and attitudes we have toward
that item, person, or experience.

To illustrate this point when I am talking to an audience, I often
hold up a styrofoam cup that I acquire with the refreshments
served just before my seminar. I ask people the correct name for
this item: "Is it a cup? Is it a container? Is it a vessel? Is it a
commercial product? Is it an achievement of modern technology? Is
it potential litter?" Then I ask them which of those terms we should
consider the one, single, and only correct label. Invariably someone
chuckles, "All of the above!" And I respond, "Exactly!"

So it is with the experiences in our lives. We can choose to call
them many different things, and what we call them determines

how we relate to them. Calling an experience by a new yet valid name, instead of one we have previously been using, often frees us to approach it in an entirely new way and to feel much better about it. This therapeutic procedure is "reframing."

You look at a small, white-bordered photograph of a loved one and consider it a lovely "snapshot." You have it enlarged and set into an expensive gold frame. Now you call it a "portrait." The same picture reframed holds new significance for you.

In the example at the beginning of this chapter, I reframed the telephone caller's hardship into "opportunity." Note that I did not deny his heartbreak. Reframing does not whitewash. I do not pretend that something is *other* than what the sufferer thinks, but I point out what else it is *besides* the intolerable experience that the person's original label makes it.

I have heard that the word in Chinese picture writing for "crisis" combines the pictures for two other words: "danger" and "opportunity." When a man concentrates only on the danger aspect of a crisis, he feels frightened, paralyzed into spinning his wheels in uncreative anguish. When instead he focuses his primary attention on the opportunity aspect, he triggers a whole dimension of resourcefulness in himself that he is already familiar with using in challenging situations that interest him. As mentioned in chapter 2 ("Transfer"), the ability to become interested, curious, diligent, and persistent in *some* circumstances is the vitality that counselors want desperately to arouse in clients toward the troublesome circumstances that prompt them to seek help.

Probably my primary goal in brief therapy is to release that vitality in an abrupt manner by helping people to see their situations differently. I have achieved that goal when people say thoughtfully, "I never looked at it that way before." I know then that I have helped them to see with new eyes. I have the satisfaction of knowing that in some small degree I have been the light of the world to dispel some of the darkness that men so often embrace rather than light (John 3:19).

## Labels as Keys

When people feel stuck in a particular situation, they approach life as if they find all doors locked. A novel label for the troublesome situation often becomes a key that unlocks at least one door and frees a person from indecision.

In his classic book *Principles of Psychology,* William James says that we often move out of indecision upon ". . . . the discovery that we can refer the case to a *class* upon which we are accustomed to act unhesitatingly. . ." (James 1890, 430). The apostle Paul applied the same principle to relieve the frustration that Christian slaves felt about their work. He helped them to see it as merely one case of a larger class of activity familiar and exhilarating to them: worship. "Whatever you do, work at it with all your heart, as working for the Lord, not for men. . . . It is the Lord Christ you are serving" (Col. 3:23–24).

The larger a set of keys you have, the greater the chance that you can unlock a door. So I sprinkle alternative labels abundantly into the normal course of my dialogue with clients. When one key happens to work, I recognize it by a startled look of insight on the person's face, followed by some sort of appreciative, pensive remark, like, "Hey, that's it!" or "I never thought of it that way before," or "Hmm, I guess you *could* put it that way."

I major in labels that express positive character traits, words that suggest persistence, durability, sensitivity, eagerness, and yearning. For example, a man complains to me in front of his wife about her daily nagging that he ought to get a better job. I respond sympathetically by saying, "You sound like you're nearly tuckered out by her persistent encouragement toward such a lofty ambition for you." While acknowledging the husband's exhaustion, I manage with the same sentence to compliment the wife four times! I call her *persistent,* an *encourager,* one who stimulates her husband's *ambition* toward a *lofty* vision she holds for him. I might also turn to the wife and ask if she could go a little easier on her *devotion* to her husband's success.

Using the same principle, to an unmarried woman who tolerates abuse from a man she lives with, I might remark, "I am impressed at your durability." She may accept that reframe (in place of seeing herself as "cowardly") and decide she is *durable* enough to live without this illicit lover.

Consider the case of a businessman who promises too many jobs to his customers because he fears their displeasure if he says, "I'm sorry. I'm already booked solid." I tell him that I marvel at his uncommon *sensitivity* to the feelings of his fellowman. Or I muse, "So, your *compassion* sometimes gets in your way." Or I might quip, "Blessed are the *merciful,*" or ask, "In other words, is *being gentle* one of your highest priorities?" Perhaps I speculate: *"Protecting other people that way must be quite a burden for you."*

If a married couple starts to bicker in front of me after blaming each other for their communication problems, I might interrupt by saying, "I am deeply moved by the intensity of your *eagerness* to get through to each other on a really satisfying level of *heartfelt* human contact. Why, just look at the energy you are both pouring into this conversation right now! Now tell me, what will be the first encouraging sign to you that this kind of *investment* is beginning to pay off?"

With the same couple I might also try to reorient them by arousing their curiosity: "Do you know that your fighting tells me something precious about you guys? The depth of your emotional pain is a direct measure of your *yearning* for a safe, tender, respectful relationship between you." Since the flip side of what they complain about tells me what they hunger for, I put that into positive words and praise them for it.

I sometimes use yet another reframe with couples who fight so intensely in my presence that I have a hard time breaking into their conversation. Nevertheless, I *do* break in, emphatically, and redirect them with something like this:

> Hold it! Hold it! Whoa! Stop! This is fantastic! Do you realize what's going on here? I am a pretty forceful guy and yet I have been trying unsuccessfully to get a word in edgewise with you people. I could not pry your attention away from each other. You have been absolutely *riveted on each other* for the past half minute. You know, hate and anger are not the opposite of love—indifference is. And you two are obviously not indifferent to each other. More than anything else in the world, you each wanted to get through to the other. I call that *involvement.*

Again, the purpose of reframing is not to whitewash horrible things, but to see them in a new light that makes them not merely horrible, but also workable.

## Hardships as Opportunities

I have already mentioned the general relabeling of hardships as opportunities. The next several paragraphs present some positive ways to construe hardships with the catchy phrases or memorable word pictures conveyed by particular labels. People often come back weeks, months, or even years after a therapeutic encounter with me and say that a particular reframing phrase had stuck with them and served as a touchstone to get them through difficult situations. I will describe several such in the next section.

*"Labor pains."* I frequently tell people after they describe a difficult situation they are going through that their pain is not pointless. I say, "Your pains are labor pains—something new is being born within you." This arouses in them a sense of meaning, purpose, and value about their ordeal. They can see it as personal inner-growth time, not useless suffering.

*"Innoculation."* This concept is particularly good to use when comforting a child who has just been disappointed, or when counseling an adult with whom you are discussing childhood hurts. For example, a junior-high boy tries out for a team at school and fails to make it. After listening, you tell him that in a way he is more fortunate than a lot of other kids. You pause at that point to let his curiosity develop. Then you tell him that young people who always have things go their way and don't meet their first disappointments until adulthood are really going to have a rough time later on. They are like adults who were not "fortunate" enough to get mumps as children. An adult who catches mumps suffers from it far worse than a child would. In the same way, small doses of emotional hurt can serve as vaccinations early in life, allowing our psychological systems to develop antibodies that protect us later on against debilitating doses of that affliction.

Youngsters who never experience disappointment or rejection or frustration enter adult life far too vulnerable to difficulties. Someone who faced a particular trouble as a kid can say, when coming upon it again in adult life, "I know how to handle this. I've been here before." The person without such an immunity will usually feel not just diappointed, but devastated. A counselor can help reframe painful disappointments so that they no longer seem like the end of all things worth living for, but rather *preparation* for future joys even more worthwhile. Reorienting toward the future often marks a major step in recovering from depression.

Relabeling disappointment or abandonment or abuse as a "childhood disease" indirectly gives people several healthy options:

1. The reference to "childhood" means the hurt was temporary. Much of what psychotherapists deal with is unfinished business. When a person rethinks the time of childhood difficulty, the concept that "this, too, will pass" is central to the finishing process.

2. Calling it "a disease" implies a cure. People already carry in their minds a precedent for having undergone and recovered from physical diseases.

3. The disease label also normalizes the experiences. You consider a person an oddity if he or she never had a childhood disease: "That poor kid was probably overprotected—not one of us 'normal' people." Therefore, this view moves the problem out of the category of resented unfinished business and puts it into the category of the testing-by-fire that makes a war veteran.

*"Boot camp."* I often refer to times of testing as preparations for future usefulness, much like soldiers learn combat skills by going through the rigors of boot camp. Similarly, athletes develop strength and endurance on the practice field and train in gymnasiums by going through stressful activities. Both groups put themselves into diligent training under a trusted drill instructor, or coach.

Incidentally, where the Bible refers to the Lord as "Shepherd," we might plug in a more familiar twentieth-century American metaphor—that of "Coach." In either capacity, a protector devotes himself to the well-being and future development of the persons entrusted to his care. Even when subjecting his charges to difficulty, the divine Shepherd/Coach has in mind a future objective impossible for the sheep/child/athlete to fully grasp and appreciate in that moment of pain.

I often talk about clients developing "inner muscle," referring to godly character traits that only suffering can develop. The most obvious such trait is longsuffering, or patience. In our areas of immaturity, we typically favor short suffering. We want our difficulties over with quickly since we tolerate little frustration and want instant results. The result is that we often fail to persist in directions that would benefit us if only we continue long enough.

Suffering also serves to develop within us compassion for anyone else who undergoes such pain. People often respond well to the motto, "something good is happening," even as they are undergoing hardship. A Scripture passage that phrases this particularly well refers to ". . . the Father of compassion and the God of all comfort, who comforts us in all our troubles, so that we can comfort those in any trouble with the comfort we ourselves have received from God" (2 Cor. 1:3–4).

Continuing to *endure* suffering, rather than running away from it or having a temper tantrum, helps to develop the inner muscle of self-control. Thus it is particularly to be welcomed by those who have difficulties with impulse control, who readily throw up their hands and quit when discouraged. Or those who lash out at people or things when feeling frustrated at not solving their difficulties quickly and easily on the first try.

*Thanksgiving.* To transform people's irritations, I take seriously the Scripture that says, "Give thanks in all circumstances, for this is God's will for you in Christ Jesus" (1 Thess. 5:18). To get clients to do this task—which they could readily resist—I reframe it as a powerful exercise in faith. I tell them that if I deliberately thank God for some hardship I am suffering, which I don't *feel* like doing, I am exercising obedience to God in a high degree. My motivation is strictly to praise him, and I *choose* to do it. How different from doing something I can hardly help doing when I feel great and bubble over with enthusiasm! I explain that giving thanks acknowledges God's good character, regardless of our liking for our current circumstances.

Thanksgiving makes a down payment on future joy. I affirm that God is wise enough to know what I am going through, powerful enough to change my circumstances if he wanted to, and good enough to do what is best for me whether or not it is what *I* want. By thanking him for permitting this unpleasant circumstance to continue in my life, I remind myself that I believe God knows what he is doing, even when I don't yet know what he is doing or why.

By taking that first step, thanking God even when I don't *feel* thankful, I free myself from the bitterness that paralyzes my creativity. Then I can examine myself to detect anything I did or neglected to do that brought this suffering on me as a natural consequence of my own foolishness. In this case I have a marvelous opportunity to learn from a difficult experience and improve myself. And I can certainly feel thankful about that!

When I don't see any error on my part to account for my hardship, I turn to ponder what my powerful, wise, and good God has in mind in allowing it to occur. As I catch a glimpse of my increased future usefulness to his kingdom, I welcome the chance to have refined like gold in a crucible such godly character traits as "compassion, kindness, humility, gentleness and patience" (Col. 3:12).

"The *binocular trick.*" I tell people sometimes that when they look at their difficulties, they magnify them as if viewing them through binoculars, making them larger than life. By contrast, when they look at their ability to handle their difficulties, they switch the binoculars around and look through the wrong end, so that they make far too little of their resourcefulness. I borrow this concept from Dr. David Burns, author of *Feeling Good* (1980, 36), a best-selling self-help book for curing depression by cognitive therapy.

I cast the idea into a biblical frame by urging the client to do as the psalmist says: "Glorify the Lord with me. . ." (Ps. 34:3). I urge them when feeling down or preoccupied with their painful circumstances to imagine that they swing a set of binoculars away from trouble and onto something about God that they deeply admire and find glorious. I tell them to see that attribute getting larger and lovelier. Then I have them switch the binoculars around and look back at their troubles, now seeing them small in comparison with God's glory and their own capabilities as creatures made in the image of this glorious God.

*Romans 8:28 and 29.* Well-meaning but ineffectual friends who try to counsel persons in difficulty often glibly quote Romans 8:28: "And we know that in all things God works for the good of those who love him, who have been called according to his purpose." This attempt to comfort often fails because people attribute such a vague and far-off "purpose" to God. But "the good" that he has in mind comes out clearly in the subsequent verse: ". . . to be conformed to the likeness of his Son. . . ."

So there I have a scriptural quotation with which I encourage people. I can say with genuine enthusiasm, "God has a project underway in your life that was the whole point of his making creation in the first place, and then tolerating it when it deviated from his original perfect plan. He is using every circumstance in your life for your good. That means for nothing less than to mold and shape in you a character identical to that in the Lord Jesus Christ himself!"

This approach fits especially well with people who sigh half-heartedly about their troubles, "Well, I know that God is working all things together for good in my life, *but*. . . ." I rush in to tell them, "You didn't go far enough!" Having thus aroused their curiosity, I proceed with the above pep talk, tailored for the individual I am counseling.

*Curiosity.* People tolerate suffering better when they become *observers* as well as *participants*. Anthropologists often study aboriginal tribes by making themselves participant-observers. That means they watch and record what they are doing while they are interacting with the tribal people. I often assign people to the role of non-miserable "researcher" when I send them back to their un-changed, miserable situations. I might even urge them to write down, and bring to me the next time we meet, three particular things they learned about this kind of experience or about them-selves as revealed in their school of hard knocks.

Consistent with the earlier concept of comforting others with the same comfort that we ourselves have received from God, I urge people not to miss the opportunity to taste their particular pain thoroughly and fully. Since such feelings as loneliness, inadequacy, helplessness, bereavement, and anxiety are common human expe-riences, we can enter into the full mainstream of the human drama by drinking our sorrows to the dregs. Going through an experience with full awareness, not blunting it with mere teeth-gritting toler-ation, we put ourselves in a position to say, "So this is what it's like." We no longer need dictionary definitions of words like "disappointment" or "heartache" if we know these experiences in our own hearts.

*Worship.* A Christian man once complained to me that he had worked long and carefully to put up some paneling in the family room of their home because his wife wanted it done. He did it as a favor to her, eager for her to show delight. To his consternation, she did not like it when she saw it finished, and insisted that he tear it down. As he tore it down, he resented all the work he had put into it. He came to me with angry feelings about all that "wasted time."

I told him that he reminded me of a certain priest in ancient Israel. As I have demonstrated a number of times in this book, I often like to say things in an intriguing way. By this technique I redirect the grinding momentum of people's negative feeling into a forward-moving emotional condition, which is one way to accom-plish reframing. In the present case, having told the man that he reminded me of a priest in Israel, I had his undivided attention. He was all ears to make sense of what I could possibly mean and how it applied to his situation. Teachers speak of this as a "teachable moment."

I proceeded to say that the priest in Israel "wasted" bulls, lambs, and rams by burning them on the altar as worshipful sacrifices to God. Since this devout man did not think of *those* sacrifices as "wasted," *his* time in the basement might not be considered "wasted" if he could view it in some way as a worshipful sacrifice to God.

Next I used that lovely reframe I mentioned earlier in this book, Colossians 3:23, written to slaves: "Whatever you do, work at it with all your heart, as working for the Lord, not for men"—"or for a wife," I interjected. Then I jumped to the end of verse 24 and added, "It is the Lord Christ you are serving." The inconvenience this twentieth-century saint suffered in his family room was no longer seen as fruitless suffering at the hands of a faulty loved one. It became a reverent sacrifice to a magnificent God who loves them both.

*The friction principle.* Suppose a woman comes to me greatly upset about "friction" in some relationship, such as with a spouse or an elderly parent or a teenage child. The client is a Pleaser, allergic to interpersonal conflict and wanting peace at any price. I talk to her about the benefits of friction. I use the analogy of a car on an icy road, where there is so little friction between tire and road that the car goes nowhere or skids aimlessly. I emphasize, "It is only friction that makes controlled movement possible." I tell her that nothing would ever improve if she could please everybody all the time. I say, "Friction allows directed movement on the road— and in the home."

*"Music to my ears."* A mother of twin toddlers complained that she was at her wit's end when either of the kids cried. She was so conscientious that she took their crying as a sign of her failure. She also felt guilty for resenting the noise. I had to figure some way to get her to view the crying as a positive sign, neither a condemnation of her nor an unjust ordeal.

I asked this mother to imagine that a terrible tragedy had happened, to suppose there was a fire in the house and she was not able to get to the twins' bedroom and they died a terrible death. I asked how she would feel. Horrified, she said that she would feel awful and would miss the twins terribly. I then asked her to imagine that by magic she could restore the situation to the way it was before, with her house intact and with the twins still in it, except on one condition—that the kids be allowed to cry. I asked how she would feel about their crying then. She laughed and said, "It would be music to my ears." I then looked her in the eye and asked, "Is there any reason it cannot be now?" Those were her own words: "Music to my ears." She wrote them on a slip of paper, which she put on her refrigerator, and looked at every time she felt exasperated by a chorus of crying.

The next time we talked, she told me that this motto had greatly reduced her feeling of resentment and emotional bondage when the kids cried. I went a step further to attach additional positive meaning to that trying experience. I asked her if she ever had difficulty telling her identical twins apart. She told me several idiosyncrasies of each by which she distinguished them. I said, "Now here you have a marvelous opportunity to add another mark of individuality to your repertoire. Listen carefully to notice how each one's cry differs from the other's. Whenever either one is crying, notice that child's unique 'signature.'"

## Reframing the Motivation of Others

In one of the most powerful mind-renewals I do, I reframe the "villains" or troublesome characters in clients' lives as frightened, wounded, crippled, weak, and needy persons. When I explain their irregular behaviors as awkward or clumsy signs of deficiency, I am debunking clients' view that these "wrongdoers" are powerful, coordinated, skillful, self-assured, and/or poised perpetrators of intentional malice.

When clients make that transition, they typically feel sorry for persons they had formerly feared or resented. The sound psychological principle they adopt finds its roots in Scripture: "There is no fear in love. But perfect love drives out fear . . ." (1 John 4:18). "Perfect love" really means love that is perfect-*ed,* mature, complete, and it generally takes the form of compassion. I seek to arouse feelings of compassion in clients in order to dispel negative emotions of fear and its cousins: resentment, guilt, hatred, and vengeance. Sorrow and love mingle to form compassion, putting the former victim in the driver's seat for the good of the former persecutor. Below are several examples of how this is done.

*Removing the Camouflage.* A single man in his late twenties once came to tell me that he was about to visit his father, who had apparently never expressed any heartfelt love for the boy. The son said, "I feel cheated because I have never gotten my father's blessing." He then described how Dad always communicated in a bantering, joking, avoidant kind of style.

I asked the son, who was obviously very anxious to have his dad's approval, what he thought was going on inside his father when he joked like that. (Clients usually have not thought about what emotions are going on in the other person, when they themselves are preoccupied with the pain of disappointment or rejection that they feel at the hands of that other person.) The young man thought about it for a while and then said, "I guess he just thinks he's quite humorous." I said I didn't think so, that generally it's a sign of nervousness when people joke excessively. I asked the son to consider what his father might be nervous or scared about. The son couldn't come up with any idea, but I suggested that he might get a clue from his own feelings. Since the young man so urgently wanted a parental blessing, the father might fear not giving an adequate one. That is, Dad worried that his son might not welcome, appreciate, or approve what the father offered.

I suggested that Dad was essentially a shy man, scared of being thought inadequate. Then I said to the son, "I don't have any crystal ball, and I could be all wet concerning your father. But if he *were* feeling nervous about his possible inadequacy, what would you feel like doing toward him?"

The son immediately replied, "Oh, I would want to tell him, 'Dad, it's okay. Just tell me from your heart that you love me. It doesn't have to be special or perfect or done some certain way, just so it's from *you!*'" The earnestness in the young man's voice projected an entirely different way of viewing the situation than he had expressed when talking of himself as being cheated by a stingy father.

"You can learn to hear a blessing in another language than your native tongue." I told this to the son as part of helping him to understand his father's banter as the "safest" way for him to communicate affection to his son. I called it a "guarded attempt" by the father. I asked the son to forgive his father's shyness and to accept the positive intention that it camouflaged.

*"Burn victim."* My wife and I began dating each other as juniors in college, six months after a fire had burned her face and hands. One chilly fall day, we walked into a room where a fire burned in a fireplace at the far end. Ruth turned abruptly in pain, saying, "Oh, the fire, I can feel it!" I realized that the tender flesh beneath her new skin still overresponded to heat radiation that I could barely detect.

I often tell this story to people bothered by the unkind actions of an irregular person in their lives. I refer to such other persons as "burn victims," implying that they were burned in childhood by such difficult experiences as humiliation, ridicule, abandonment, abuse, or any other form of rejection. I say that the hurtful actions they now indulge in are pathetic, desperate attempts to protect themselves against being burned again. These one-time victims go by the policy, "The best defense is a strong offense." The pain of their childhood burns preoccupies them so greatly that they think primarily in terms of self-protection, downplaying cooperation as an element in achieving an enjoyable relationship with another person. They focus more on the dangers of intimacy than its opportunities.

This is a particularly good reframe to use with people who live or work with unusually defensive individuals. Again, it arouses a client's compassion, so that his or her orientation is as a dedicated helper to the wounded person, rather than as a beleaguered underling.

*Test pilot.* A husband and wife came to me with their teenage foster daughter. They complained that she constantly provoked them by misbehavior and by statements like, "You don't really care what happens to me." Although they constantly reassured her to the point of their own exasperation, she rejected each of their declarations of devotion to her.

I asked the three of them if they had seen a movie that was current at the time, *The Right Stuff.* When they affirmed that they had, I asked if they remembered the sequence in which test pilot Chuck Yeager broke the sound barrier for the first time. They certainly did remember. I said that he really pushed that aircraft to its limits, not because he wanted to destroy it, but because he wanted to see how much it could handle—so that people could know how useful that design of aircraft would be.

Then I told them that I thought the foster daughter was a "test pilot." It was so important to her to know that she could rely on this pair of adults that she would use all the cleverness she could muster to discover just how reliable they were. I said I thought her motivation was not to destroy her foster parents, but to find them durable and dependable. I joked that it might feel to them as if she was trying to ruin them, but people only test the things that matter most to them. They discard the things that they find useless. I told them that this girl *wants* to rely on them. I glanced over at her and asked, "Am I right?" She blushed, grinned, shuffled her feet, and mumbled, "I guess so."

This reframe was especially valuable because it was done with the foster daughter present. It relabeled her behavior not only to the parents, but also to her. Therefore she could never again indulge in one of her provocative behaviors or statements without its reminding her of the conversation that we had about it in my office. That gave even misbehavior a whole new meaning. Now it was an act of devotion rather than defiance. I had reframed her actions as *cooperating* with the foster-parent–child process rather than fighting it.

*Translating signals correctly.* Dolores, a divorced woman, had married Andrew and brought into the marriage her eight-year-old son, Billy. Seven years later the family came to see me because of Billy's falling grades in school. Billy was obviously a bright kid who could do much better in school. As we probed the situation, Billy said bitterly that he never felt that Andrew had accepted him, much less loved him as a son.

Andrew had tried hard to be a good stepfather, but he did this mostly by checking up on Billy to be sure he completed chores, by riding him for getting poor grades in school, and by insisting that he could do better. Dad mistakenly emphasized criticism and punishment at the expense of expressing praise and affection. In cases like this—with a bright teenager older than about fourteen—you can often accomplish the fastest positive improvement by focusing your attention on renewing the mind of the young person.

So here was Billy, aggrieved at the inadequate behavior of his well-meaning stepfather. I asked Billy why he thought "Dad" had never told him straight out, "I love you." Billy said he was pretty sure it was because Andrew did *not* love him. I answered that I was not so sure of that and in fact I had a quite different idea. I asked Billy, "Could it be that Andrew is not sure if *you* have ever accepted *him?*" Billy was dumbfounded. Before he could say anything further, I asked him, "Have you ever looked at this marriage through Andrew's eyes? Here he comes into a family where the woman wanted him, but he wasn't at all sure that he could win her boy over. Maybe Andrew is a sensitive guy who would feel devastated if he told you his real feelings of affection and you said that you were not interested. Did you ever stop to think that it might be such a painful blow to Andrew that he would rather not risk it?"

Billy looked over at his stepfather cautiously. Andrew met his

gaze, and they both smiled nervously. Andrew's eyes were glisten-
ing, and that said it all. Then Andrew spoke straight out, "I *do* love
you, Billy."

*Attack means desire.* An elderly conflict-prone couple sat down to
talk to me about how much trouble they had getting along with
each other. Before we talked half an hour I had to interrupt their
bickering pattern several times. One would make an innocent observation or express mild displeasure in the form of an indirect
remark that the other could interpret in a couple of possible ways.
The other would consistently announce what the remark meant
and insist that the partner had intended it to hurt.

I finally decided to intervene by helping them to reframe one of
these double messages lovingly. The sequence went like this:

> *Wife* (to husband): "You're not saying very much today."
>
> *Husband* (with mixed cynicism and discouragement): "Well, my
> opinion never seems to count for much anyway."
>
> *Wife* (to counselor, irate): "See there, he's blaming me for all our
> problems. I just hate it when he jabs at me like that."
>
> *Counselor* (to wife): "You know, a question just came to me. Why
> do you suppose your husband spoke like that? What was going
> on inside him? What did it do *for* him to speak that way *to*
> you?"
>
> *Wife:* "I don't know."
>
> *Counselor:* "Well, I think he's being cautious. He did not come
> out and say directly that he dearly wants to know that his
> opinions matter to you. So he hinted at it, as if it were too
> dangerous a remark. Maybe he feels that to say it in a vulnera-
> ble and tender way would leave him completely unprotected if
> you would happen to say that his opinions do *not* matter to
> you. So I see him wording things in a tough-sounding way to
> protect himself against the fate he fears worse than death,
> namely . . . the loss of *your* esteem."

Even when I meet with only one member of a troubled relationship, I usually choose the above point of view. It helps to
sweeten and vitalize both parties, as well as *me,* when I reframe a
nasty action as a proof of love. I naturally tend to feel somewhat
discouraged or even argumentative when I view a client's nasty
remark as nothing but a vicious attempt to destroy another person.

But I brim with tenderness toward a couple and feel eager optimism for their future if I can reframe an offender's negative behavior as a desperate effort at self-protection against being rejected by the partner. This thereby shows how extremely important to the offender is his or her victim's acceptance. Jabs and innuendoes in conflicts between loved ones are often cautious attempts to communicate. Loved ones have more power to hurt us by rejection than do any battalion of enemies whose opinions mean nothing to us.

People to whom I offer this reframe sometimes modify it by referring henceforth to the cryptic double messages as "defensiveness." That adequately embraces my goals, which are (1) to turn people from seeing the remarks as cruel attacks; and (2) to tickle the recurrent new thought "my partner is afraid of losing my love."

Sometimes, with a couple (or with a parent and child), after I have given the reframe to the wounded one, I turn to the offender and say, "Tell your partner that you urgently hunger to be in her [his] good favor." Generally, if my suggestion is followed, the partner answers lovingly and they tearfully embrace. This happens even with people who shrieked angrily at each other only five minutes earlier! Truly, we are *transformed* by the renewing of our minds. (A later chapter discusses what to do when people do *not* smoothly cooperate with a loving recommendation like the above).

## "It *Could* Be Worse"

When people talk about things that are going sour in their lives, I sometimes reminisce to them about a vow that I once made when in great pain in a hospital bed. I vowed that if I was ever free from this pain, I would always appreciate that simple fact, no matter what else was going on in my life. I tell clients that in that extremity of pain I touched a kind of bedrock by which I measure almost anything else as something worth appreciating because "at least I am not in pain." Then I ask them if they have ever had a similar experience, compared to which they would welcome *anything* else in their lives—including the unpleasant circumstances that now bring them to talk to me. This, too, is reframing, since it in effect views an albeit unpleasant situation as "not the worst thing that could happen."

*Do a blessing count.* I often use a personal anecdote about my aggravation while driving in a traffic jam. People who talk about frustrations, inconveniences, and irritations almost always identify traffic as a prime "pet peeve." I tell how I felt impatient when cars were just creeping along during a particular rush hour when I wanted to get somewhere in a hurry. A highway construction project made the jam even worse.

In the midst of this frustration I suddenly did something to vault myself out of that negative frame of mind. I asked myself how else I could look at the situation. What kind of *good* things were causing this *bad* situation? It dawned on me that the reason I was in a traffic jam was that I lived in a prosperous nation presently at peace, so that almost every residence in my fortunate community had at least one car! The traffic also crowded the highways because there were no secret police detaining people and no concentration camps keeping some of them off the streets. In fact, this construction project gave evidence that we lived under a government honest enough to direct tax money toward the public good! By reminding myself that not all nations were so lucky, I decided that I had pretty luxurious problems.

I use this story to teach people to follow the concept in the gospel song: "Count Your Blessings, Name Them One by One." I ask people to enumerate the things that *are* going well in their lives. This works particularly well with highly responsive people who simply have the bad habit of frequently getting annoyed by the minor inconveniences of everyday living. Such people often respond well to slogans, particularly if they also happen to attend self-help groups like Alcoholics Anonymous or AlAnon. I remind them of the familiar saying: "I felt sorry for myself because I had no shoes, until I saw a man who had no feet."

*"What's going right?"* Sometimes, after people rattle off to me a list of many things that are going wrong and we have talked about these a while, I kind of lean back and say, "You know, we have talked a lot about what's going *wrong* in your life. And there certainly is much of that. But let's shift gears for a moment and let you tell me what is going right. What are some things that are happening that you want to continue to have happen?" Clients usually act a little bewildered at this change of pace and need some prodding from me. So I ask a couple of questions about extreme conditions that I am pretty sure do *not* apply. Of a couple that I

suspect never go beyond raising their voices, I might ask, "Well, for example do the two of you hit each other when you have arguments?" They immediately say something like, "Oh, no. We would never do that!" Then I point that out as one good item on their list and lead the discussion into how far they want to continue that self-control, which they have already established in their relationship.

I go on to help such a couple formulate a list that reflects the fact that they occasionally *do* spend some enjoyable time together. These golden nuggets almost automatically become things that they decide to do more of in the near future. Typically they come back to me a week later saying that they did one or two items that they hadn't done in a long time and really enjoyed themselves. The purpose of this kind of intervention is to get people thinking in terms of positive possibilities, to help them envision a workable future, preferably by using their own ideas.

*Don't minimize the bad.* One caution with this accentuate-the-positive technique is to avoid a superficial, cheerleader kind of approach. As counselor I want to convey to people that things really could be worse, that in fact—given the circumstances—it's amazing that things in their lives are as *good* as they are. I muse to them that they must be doing *something* right!

With people who talk about suicide, I ask what has kept them from killing themselves so far, hoping to draw out very clearly their interest in life. With couples who talk about divorce, I compliment them for seeking counsel and ask why they *have* stayed together. A superficial pep talk merely minimizes how bad things are. Instead, what I do is try to maximize how fortunate or competent the clients are. I want to arouse either gratitude or confidence or both, in place of negative emotions of resentment and discouragement.

## A Touch of Kind Humor

In each of the next four examples, I take a lighthearted approach as therapist. Just as a political cartoonist caricatures some feature of a personage, I sometimes take small elements within the situations that clients present to me and blow them out of proportion. This brings in the relief of humor and the clear-thinking perspective that absurdity often lends by its contrast with the more moderate nature of most things in our lives. *I am careful not to be sarcastic,* but merely playful, since sarcasm conveys a double message. Although it uses a friendly format of humor, it has buried within it a hurtful barb. Jesus said, "Let your yes be yes and your no be no," but sarcasm gives a yes/no mixed message. It tends to distance clients, rather than building trust and rapport in the counseling situation.

Carefully designed offhand, whimsical comments helps diminish the grimness of situations that people bring to me, without discounting the seriousness of their suffering. In the first example below, a lighthearted phrase "Army buddies," served to thaw a man's emotional rigidity into a tenderhearted expression of sadness he really did feel very deeply.

Part of the effectiveness of the gently humorous phrases that I call "quips," is that they come into therapy on the backstroke. They are little give-aways. Because they come out in a joking context, I seem not to be doing therapy at the moment, but simply conversing. They have a quality of "this one doesn't count," so resistant clients, who seem to have the front door to their understanding barred, can let this kind of indirect therapeutic intervention come in through the back door. I generally pepper this kind of remark freely throughout most sessions, particularly with boisterous clients, but I go easy on humor with people who seem devoted to creating a grim climate with me.

*Army buddies.* I urged one obsessive man to openly grieve some recent losses, including his young adult son who had moved out of the house. The man pretended not to have any feelings about that loss, even though he and his son had lived together for some years after the death of the boy's mother when he was seven years old. The man asked me why he should cry. I said it was part of the healing process to express grief over the friendships he had lost recently—his parents, both of whom had died a few months before, and his son who had moved out. "After all," I said, "You guys were Army buddies." The man laughed and said, "That's right. We went through the war together." And his eyes moistened.

*The strong-willed grandmother.* A husband and wife talked with me about difficulties they were having with the wife's mother, who insisted that they use certain child-rearing techniques on her grandchild of which this husband and wife did not approve. As they described these clashes with Grandmother, I commented, "Sounds like maybe Jim Dobson needs to write another book, entitled *The*

*Strong-Willed Grandmother."* The husband and wife laughed heartily, saying, "That's it! That's it!" It helped them see Grandma as handicapped rather than domineering.

*"Ultimatum foreplay."* Another husband and wife talked about the difficulty they were having getting together sexually. The husband tended to withdraw from his wife much of the time. Since the wife usually waited for him to approach her, she would often get so disgusted that she would say angrily that either they were going to have an intimate relationship or none at all. Whenever she acted as if she was ready to end the marriage, the husband became quite warm and tender and they had great sex. I commented that this interesting new procedure should appear in the sex manuals, and we could perhaps call it "ultimatum foreplay."

*"Gary Poppins."* A male client Gary told me about his relationship with his wife. She worked as the breadwinner, and he concentrated on raising the kids and taking care of the household. He mentioned all of this in the context of feeling unappreciated for doing a lot that most men would refuse to do. I casually remarked to him, "So you're a regular Gary Poppins, eh?"

## Using Memorable Images

In brief therapy you want a few impactful things to really stick in the person's mind. Memory systems emphasize the value of mental pictures to associate with the things we want to remember. Mental pictures and associations become most memorable when we make them bizarre, dramatic, shocking, ludicrous, or highly colorful.

I regularly use this idea to remember where I set down my eyeglasses. Anytime that I just leave them somewhere without making a special mental note of it, I have to go through an entire house search to locate them. I can save myself this inconvenience by making a mental note associated with a vivid picture. For example, if I set them down on the piano, I picture myself having slammed them down much too hard, so that they shatter into jagged sharp pieces that cut my hand and that blood runs all over the piano as from a fire hydrant. Of course, one of the great values of mental imagery is that we don't have to go through the actual experience that we can imagine! But by creating a mental picture so alarming and potentially painful, I have no problem remembering later in the day where I left my glasses.

In my counseling, especially with my quips, I try to put in little mental snapshots. I load my remarks with offbeat visual imagery and picturesque language. People often repeat such comments to me weeks or months later and mention their having helped them, somewhat like keys that unlocked certain doors in their lives.

*The hibernating wife.* One man told about his wife's shy and distrustful manner. During counseling we discovered that this withdrawing tendency on her part probably began long before she met her husband. This woman had grown up under icy blasts of criticism from her parents, who often said such things as, "Oh, you'll never amount to anything."

I referred to this man's wife as having "gone into hibernation" as a child to survive those icy blasts. The concept stuck with the man. When he thought of his wife as "hibernating," rather than as avoiding him or disliking him, his whole mood toward her changed. First of all, he saw her withdrawn shyness as an action to protect herself, not to frustrate him—so he felt compassion rather than irritation toward her. Second, since the concept of hibernation implies a *temporary* condition, I had taken pains not to describe the wife's trust as having "died" in childhood. This set a challenging possibility before this husband. To say it in metaphorical language, he could create a spring sunshine of marital affection that would thaw the ice in his wife's heart and waken her from a long winter's sleep.

*Turnabout.* With another couple, I saw a typical pattern in their behavior. The depressed husband repeatedly put himself down with remarks like, "I'm no good for anything. I can't see why my wife puts up with me." Each time, the wife rushed in to offer sympathetic words like, "Oh, honey, you shouldn't be so hard on yourself." Immediately after she did that during one counseling session, I told her I wanted to give her some different words to try. I coached her to tell her husband, "Don't insult me. Don't give people the idea that I married a dummy." This novel rebuke intrigued both of them. The wife said, "I never thought of it that way before, but when he puts himself down he *does* make me look like a fool for having married him. So his self-criticism criticizes me, too."

This couple would never again repeat their old automatic pattern. Our novel and somewhat humorous discussion made it forever impossible for them to start acting out their time-worn scenario without remembering the conversation about it in my office. By removing one little piece of dysfunctional behavior, they had more time and energy available for creative alternatives.

*"There I go again!"* I often recommend to people who want to change a bad habit that they adopt a playful inner sentence, "There I go again!" each time they notice themselves doing the "forbidden" behavior. Typically, obsessive and perfectionistic people mentally flog themselves whenever they notice themselves repeating the bad habit. But that personal whipping feeds their grim approach and simply entrenches them in the gloom and depression that so often accompany obsessions. "There I go again!" offers a more offhanded, whimsical observation of the bad habit. The memorable phrase *frees* people to change their behavior, rather than coercing them to do so. It triggers a sense of adventure, since it implies, "I wonder what else I could do instead."

One man put this sentence into operation whenever he fell into his old bad habit of overreacting to his wife's accusations. Since he typically defended himself by explaining and justifying his actions, his wife rarely felt that he heard and understood where she was coming from. I told this man that he had an overly sensitive mental smoke alarm that went off as if the house were on fire, whereas all that happened was that somebody blew out a birthday candle. This image symbolized his excessive reaction to the rather small assaults his wife made on him. This man, whose name was Smith, decided to laugh at himself the next time he overreacted, and to say, "There I go again, old Smokey Smitty!" (A different husband, who often blew up with a bad temper, adopted the same smoke-alarm concept and decided to refer to himself as "Smokey the Bear.")

*Hobby.* Some of the best problems to handle with memorable word pictures are little annoyances that people mention with considerable embarrassment, in almost a confessional way. These incidentals do not relate significantly to the central issue for which the people seek counseling. But clients often feel quite concerned about them and regard them as signs of deeper pathology. These minor problems are good ones to "dismiss" with an offhanded label that puts them into a much more benign category than the people fear.

For example, an obsessive young woman came to me for help with her phobia about flying in airplanes. In our second or third session, she mentioned, "Oh, by the way, I also have this weird habit of having to count all the cracks in the sidewalk when I walk from my house down to the mailbox. Does that mean I'm crazy or something?" I leaned back in my chair and with a shrug said, "Well, everybody needs a hobby." She laughed with considerable relief and repeated several times the word *hobby*. As far as I knew, She no longer expressed concern about that particular mannerism. Viewing it as a "hobby" gave her a greater freedom of choice about the compulsion, since she could either do it for recreation or decide, "I don't want to bother to do it today."

Another woman complained about her tendency to feel personally responsible and even guilty when fellow employees clashed with each other at her place of work. She said that she couldn't help taking on their burden even though she knew rationally that she was not at fault or even involved. I said, "In other words, it's kind of a hobby for you." She gasped, bewildered, "A hobby! How can you call it a hobby? It's no fun at all." I answered, "Well, it's an activity in which you invest time and energy without pay and without anyone asking you to. That's the definition of an avocation, a hobby." (A minute later I also shared with her the definition of worry as "taking on responsibilities that God never intended us to have.")

The label "hobby," with the above rationale, fits a number of annoying and nonproductive habits that people suffer over, including worries, obsessions, and compulsions. I went a step further with the above woman, since she mentioned having felt similar guilt as a child when her alcoholic parents fought. I told her that many adults tend to become fascinated with difficulties that frustrated or frightened them in childhood. Her lifelong "hobby" represented an understandable attempt to finally master something that had at one time challenged her, yet defeated her best efforts. I added, "That's why some adults like to scare themselves safely by reading horror stories." She laughed and said that that actually *was* her favorite hobby!

"*Don't have a goat. . . .*" A man with temper problems spoke with annoyance about the way his wife always started the car. He added, "That just gets my goat." I told him, "Don't have a goat—but a lamb." This man, I knew, was a devoted Christian to whom the word *lamb* conveyed special reverence for Christ. A kind of dawn came across his face as he said, "You know you're right. The way I treat my wife is really the way I am treating Jesus." That switch of one animal name for another became a small memory device that he used every time he felt annoyance rising up within him.

*The four-letter word.* When a woman comes to me for counseling, I usually ask her occupation. If she says, "Oh, I'm just a housewife," I immediately tell her, "That's a four-letter word!" I go on to describe the word *just* as an obscenity whenever it diminishes the glory of God as shown in the dignity of a person made in his image. This is particularly effective with a woman who shows by her manner and fastidious grooming that she is a person who would never use foul language. Since I want to make her self-putdown as unacceptable to her as possible, I chip away at her tendency to false humility, which is so characteristic of shy types of obsessive persons.

Now suppose a more "liberated" client tried to justify leaving her husband by saying, "I just want to find myself." In this case I might be a bit more confrontive as I refer to "just" as a four-letter word. By using the word, this careless woman minimizes the devastating seriousness of disloyalty to one's wedding vows. The most obscene words in any language are those that make fun of or discredit things having to do with either God or with very private human functions—precisely the things that we ought to treat with the most deference and courtesy.

At the opposite end of the spectrum are the obsessive persons who confide that they have probably committed "the unpardonable sin." I answer, "*You* hardly qualify!" When they ask what I mean, I tell them that the extreme anguish they feel over the possibility of having offended God certainly does not show indifference toward him. It was apathy that paralyzed the hearts of those whom Jesus warned by calling "unforgivable" their unresponsiveness to the nudging of God's Holy Spirit. And worriers about the state of their own spiritual health are anything but apathetic.

*Wounded porcupine.* A wife may come alone for marriage counseling and tell me how difficult her demanding husband is to live with. Perhaps she has been considering divorce, especially since she has asked him to come with her for counseling and he will have nothing to do with it. With such a client, I concentrate in my therapy on helping her to understand her husband's dynamics, particularly so that she can see him as crippled or handicapped. If I can arouse her compassion so that it replaces her resentment, it will give her greater strength than belligerence ever will.

I helped one such woman to think of her husband as a wounded traveler along the road of life and herself as the Good Samaritan. I suggested that although she had other business in mind, she found this needy fellow traveler and detoured from her agenda in order to seize the opportunity to apply a healing touch. No, she did not ask for or expect this encounter, I agree. But because of someone else's cruelty, her husband came into her path—wounded and in need of her compassion more than of her judgment or disappointment!

This personalized application of Christ's parable enabled the wife to view her own kind actions and helpful attitude in a fresh way. She began to see herself not as a doormat, not as a slave forced to serve a tyrant, but instead as a gifted physician treating a cut and bleeding mortal. Her focus shifted from *her* discomfort to *his*.

I referred initially to her husband as a "wounded porcupine." This helped the woman to view his belligerent, loud-voiced exterior as quills, such as a porcupine raises only when frightened. I wanted her to see his behavior as a sign of *fear* on his part, not power. After we talked about it several times, and I used enough vivid metaphors, a new automatic response developed. Now, when her husband raises his voice, she immediately thinks to herself, "The poor guy," instead of "How dare he!" She no longer takes the sting of his words upon herself, but rather sees them as expressions of *his* distress.

The porcupine analogy also helped her realize the importance of approaching her husband carefully and wisely. You don't just charge up and start doing veterinarian work on a wounded porcupine. You have to get past the quills!

*Temporary insanity.* Parents of teenagers respond particularly well to memorable word pictures or expressions that normalize the upsetting antics their kids pull. These parents often feel alone, ashamed, or blighted by a "Where did we go wrong?" oppression. When they tell about their fourteen-year-olds calling all laws "stupid" and proposing that citizens be freed from their stifling restrictions, I chuckle, "So, what's new?" I briefly comment that such trial-balloon philosophies typify the "temporary insanity" of all young people.

The exaggerated terminology helps parents to laugh with relief that (1) the condition *will* pass; and (2) it is the *kids'* ideas, not the parents', that are loony. I tell parents to welcome these outrageous philosophical pronouncements instead of opposing them in horrified overreaction. Marvelous teaching opportunities are presented when parents calmly ask such food-for-thought questions as, "Should the removal of laws include the one about driving on the right side of the road?" Parents can and should help kids *choose* values by having to think them out. For example: "If we don't have a law that cars must keep to the right of a painted line down the middle of the road, how will we keep from crashing into each other? And if we do make a law for that, how will we decide what *not* to make laws about?"

*Not "authoritarian" but "authoritative."* Sensitive parents often hesitate to firmly enforce clear household rules when their offspring violate them. Such parents hate the image of dictator or police officer that taints their concept of a person "in authority." Yet they see the need for *someone* to set limits on what young people are allowed to do.

Gentle persons in positions of authority rejoice to have two different labels to distinguish between good and bad exercises of authority. "Authoritarian" leadership is harsh, heavyhanded, inconsiderate, concerned only with compliance of the governed, not their well being. "Authoritative" means kind, clear, dependably holding firm—*because* of a concern for the well-being of the governed. A leader can be authoritative without being authoritarian.

Somewhat similarly, spiritual leaders—especially young, good-hearted pastors—often have trouble setting limits on the time they make themselves available to their parishioners. They need to see the footwashing example of Jesus in a new light. The humble disciple who occasionally sets aside the servant role is *initiating* what a particular situation calls for. That's leadership! Christlike initiative is selective and discriminating in its application. It does not follow the pattern of people who focus on prestige and approval. Its motto is: "Not the lead, but the need." Thus, the pastor's life needs some hours of *non*-availability so he or she can tend to family, study, and personal restoration.

## Storytelling

A story often helps people to identify with a hero or situation that shows a new course of action for relieving their own emotional inertia. Telling stories generally takes too long to use in brief therapy. As compared to injecting little quips and relabels, stories may interrupt the flow of counseling conversation. However, sometimes a quiet client gives you very little raw material to work with. Or an overly talkative person comes on too fast and out of sheer nervousness contributes too much superficial material. In either case, telling a story helps to control the flow of the counseling conversation and make it productive. As might be expected, I look for stories that build on raw material from the client's life.

I keep my storytelling flexible, sometimes shortening familiar tales just to make the main point. At other times I lengthen or dramatize them in order to arouse emotions that will make the point penetrate and stick with the person or will budge them past a piece of unfinished business.

The following story about Joseph represents the rather long and dramatized version. I seldom tell longer stories than this in brief therapy, although I do so in seminar presentations where I particularly wish to implant in people's minds some vivid handles by which to remember the principles I teach. I view therapy as only partly teaching, but mostly evoking from clients their own creative problem-solving capabilities. Below are eight examples of how stories can be used much like Aesop's Fables—to convey a principle:

### 1. Joseph and His Brothers:

When conversation in therapy turns to discussion of painful memories from childhood, clients typically tell of parental abuses. However, rather often the wounds came from an older brother or sister. In such cases I might tell the biblical story of Joseph from Genesis, as in this paragraph:

> Old man Jacob in the Bible had twelve sons. His favorite was Joseph. The other brothers, jealous of Joseph, mistreated him and sold him as a slave to traders who took him to Egypt. They then lied to their father that poor Joseph had been killed by wild animals. Years later these same brothers had to come down from Canaan to Egypt to get food because there was a terrible famine and Egypt was the only place in the region that had food. Egypt had planned ahead for such an emergency, due to the brilliant foresight and managerial skills of a particular man, the most powerful in all Egypt besides Pharaoh. Wouldn't you know that man turned out to be Joseph!
>
> When the brothers realized who they were dealing with and their

absolute blameworthiness before him, they were terrified. Joseph found himself in the position that victims all down through history have envied—with power to indulge vengeance upon his former persecutors. But Joseph took an amazingly different perspective. Here are his words as recorded in Genesis: "So then it was not you who sent me here, but God. . . . You intended to harm me, but God intended it for good, to accomplish what is now being done, the saving of many lives" (Gen. 45:8; 50:20).

## 2. Butterfly:

A family in my neighborhood once brought in two cocoons that were just about to hatch. They watched as the first one began to open and the butterfly inside squeezed very slowly and painfully through a tiny hole that it chewed in one end of the cocoon. After lying exhausted for about ten minutes following its agonizing emergence, the butterfly finally flew out the open window on its beautiful wings.

The family decided to help the second butterfly so that it would not have to go through such an excruciating ordeal. So, as it began to emerge, they carefully sliced open the cocoon with a razor blade, doing the equivalent of a Caesarean section. The second butterfly never did sprout wings, and in about ten minutes, instead of flying away, it quietly died.

The family asked a biologist friend to explain what had happened. The scientist said that the difficult struggle to emerge from the small hole actually pushes liquids from deep inside the butterfly's body cavity into the tiny capillaries in the wings, where they harden to complete the healthy and beautiful adult butterfly. Without the struggle, there are no wings.

I tell this story to people who are undergoing hardships, or to parents who unwisely shield their children from normal difficulties. I particularly emphasize the last line of the story: "Without the struggle, there are no wings," because I want that to sink in as a motto, as the moral of the story.

What I am doing is using the story to reframe "hardship" as the means by which we learn vitality and identity. Handling hardships does not put an end to life, but equips us for the future by showing us how to use our capabilities. With overprotective parents, I help them to see that their concern has to include the tough side of love. It certainly requires self-discipline on the part of a compassionate onlooker not to step in and try to make things easier for a struggling loved one. In the case of the butterfly, "easier" meant "fatal."

Overly kind helpers who could not restrain themselves from intervening, did not do the butterfly any favor!

### 3. The Oyster and the Pearl:

Oysters live a vulnerable existence. They have to open their tough outer shells for the necessities of eating and breathing. Each time, they expose their sensitive inner tissues to the rough particles of sand that surround them constantly. Imagine one of these jagged bits rubbing its rough corners against the soft, vulnerable flesh of the oyster's innards. You know how huge a tiny stone inside your shoe feels! Or, even worse, how a barely visible speck of grit can disable you when it gets in your eye.

How does the oyster cope? It secretes a fluid around that unwanted piece of grit. Again and again, layer upon layer, those rough edges are surrounded until finally the oyster, by thus giving something of itself, has created out of an uninvited intruder a thing of beauty and great value—a pearl.

I employ this story with people who have not yet come to terms with a past (or present) prolonged hardship that they could not escape. A woman tells me of having lived through years of physical or sexual abuse from a father, uncle, or brother. Or a man recalls boyhood years of disability with a crippled leg as he watched other kids run and play. Another might mention merciless taunting from grade-school peers for his big ears, or his funny name, or his excessive (or too little) fat.

After telling this story to such clients, I usually pause, look into their eyes, and say solemnly, "I wonder what kind of pearl was forming at that rough time in *your* life."

If a wife reports discouragement over her husband's abusive tongue, which seems constantly belittling, criticizing, and accusing her, I usually want to support her biblical obedience in staying married to this rude man. But I want to equip her to obey God *enthusiastically,* not in a morose martyrdom that dishonors God. The oyster story can give her a godly "more than conquerors" status (Rom. 8:37). This will bring her far more dignity than she could find from the secular world's remedy—the refugee status of divorcée.

I can go on to connect the oyster story to Sermon-on-the-Mount teachings like doing good to those who hurt you. The pearl comes from generous, outgoing action on the part of the oyster, which *gives* something of itself to the very object it dislikes. In a sense it thereby welcomes the uninvited grit. The oyster would create no thing of beauty if it rejected the irritant.

### 4. Undulant Fever:

My father got malaria as a young man, when a tropical mosquito bit him. Malaria is also referred to as "undulant fever," meaning that it comes and goes. The little parasites of the disease stay in your body. You can't get rid of them. You can only suppress the symptoms when they appear. Every couple of years my father had a recurrence of the symptoms—a flare-up from a bug that had bitten him years before.

I like to use this one with people who face predictable, recurring problems from a loved one. For instance, some husbands have wives who become "impossible" each month with premenstrual syndrome. Or wives of coaches "lose" their husbands at the height of certain athletic seasons. I tell these people that my father's wise employers did not take personal offense at his symptoms. They did not view his illness as disloyalty to the company or avoidance of his duties. They let him rest for a few days, until he got over the fever and returned to normal work.

Next I explore with them what kinds of "home remedies" they find generally work best to get themselves and their "feverish" loved one (and everyone else concerned) through one of those bad times, with the least upset. They typically settle on such simple ideas as having some enjoyable activities of their own to plunge into when the "malarial" loved one wants to be left alone.

The story and its funny label, "undulant fever," helps my clients to relax about their loved ones' unfriendly episodes. Their changed attitudes usually free them to entertain themselves wholeheartedly during the episodes, instead of smoldering with resentment and saying, "It's unfair," or "Last time should have been *the* last time." Knowing that the situation will come again protects them from feeling surprised or betrayed. And knowing ahead of time how they can occupy themselves during episodes makes it no longer urgent to keep the episodes from occurring.

Reframing certain unpleasant behaviors as "illness" has helped many people deal creatively with things as serious as a loved one's alcoholism. It allows them to continue loving the drinker while protecting themselves from the destructive side effects of the drunkenness. They have more options open to them than merely ending the relationship or even enduring it in quiet misery.

For the "sick" person also, viewing their condition as an illness can motivate them to manage it in ways that show consideration for other people. Of course, the "illness" reframe can backfire if people use it to escape legal or moral consequences of their inconsiderate behavior. "I'm sorry—I guess I have a bad temper" does not substitute for paying for repairs to property that one damaged in an episode of anger.

### 5. "De Gaulle Is Above!":

French General Charles De Gaulle made himself a hero of his people in World War II. Later, in a time of national crisis, they called upon him to become president. As the time for him to assume office drew near, a reporter asked him if he would lean to the political left or the right. With characteristic confidence, he quickly answered, "De Gaulle is neither left nor right. De Gaulle is above!"

This story is a useful device for people who feel themselves caught in a dilemma where they have only two options open to them: yes or no, comply or defy, frying pan or fire, damned if they do and damned if they don't. Counselors need some way to alert these people to a third dimension—General De Gaulle's "above."

Suppose a teetotaling couple wants to invite the husband's professional colleagues to their home for a party. They hesitate because all work-oriented parties they have attended have centered on alcoholic beverages. They think they must either compromise their standards or forget the party idea. Because the De Gaulle story helps them see a new dimension, they put on a wonderfully lively celebration that centers on fun activities requiring quick thinking and physical coordination—so no one there wants to be handicapped by alcohol!

### 6. Bitter or Better:

Years ago a college man and woman became engaged to be married. Two weeks before their wedding day, a tragic accident snuffed out the young woman's life. The godly college chaplain rushed to the side of the shocked husband-to-be. He told him earnestly, "Son, this experience will make you either a bitter man or a better man."

That young man did go on to become a better man. He married, raised children, and distinguished himself in compassionate Christian youth work. His ordeal typifies that inspiring quotation from Job 23:10: "But he [God] knows the way that I take; when he has tested me, I will come forth as gold."

### 7. Recalibration:

I started at left offensive tackle in the last football game of my senior year of high school. At a tense moment in the game the quarterback called a clever play: "Left tackle eligible." That meant he would throw a pass to *me*! If only I could catch the ball and not fumble it, we would probably make the eight yards we needed for a crucial first down.

As the play developed, I did catch the ball. I did hold on to it. In fact, I found myself running all alone toward the goal line with our fans cheering wildly. I was going to score a touchdown! All sorts of thoughts crowded my brain as I sprinted yard after yard down that empty gridiron. How would they word it in the headlines? Would the girls who never noticed me now treasure my merest glance? What should I do with the ball when I cross the line? But suddenly, a speedy defensive halfback from our arch-rival team ran up and tackled me from behind at about the twenty-yard line!

For days thereafter I lived in suicidal depression. I could hardly eat or sleep. I relived that run over and over again, thinking how I had blown my big chance. I could have scored my only touchdown in my whole high-school career if only I had run faster. I could have made myself a school hero, a real somebody, permanently "in."

That gloomy obsession stuck with me for thirty years until I asked myself how I could apply to it some of what I do with clients. I considered how else I could look upon that awful "failure." Suddenly it occurred to me that the purpose of the play was to gain eight yards and a first down. Well, I had succeeded in that! In fact, I had gained *forty*-eight yards and put us in great scoring position.

In the huddle as our quarterback called the play, I had chosen as my original yardstick for "success" a calibration of "catch the ball, hang on, make a first down." But in the heady excitement of dashing toward the goal line, I bumped my standard out of calibration so that only scoring a touchdown could rate as "success." Three decades later, in brief therapy on myself, I recovered vitality in a dead zone of my life by *re*-calibrating my standard back to its original setting. People, I stand here now to announce to you proudly that I *succeeded*

as a football player in my last game. After all, I got us the crucial
first down!

Achievement-oriented men often evaluate their worth in terms
of their performance. They easily lose their way when, as I did in
that football game, they substitute a *possible ideal* for a *desirable*
but realistic goal as their standard and then evaluate it as "essential." The football story calls attention to an important question:
"Hey, what was my *original* goal, and how have I done on that?"

### 8. Cornstalks:

When a farmer plants corn and it starts to grow, he must carefully
cultivate between the rows to remove weeds. Weed seeds that were in
the soil before the corn seeds were planted usually sprout faster and
grow taller than the corn in the first couple of weeks, drawing upon
essential supplies of sunshine, water, and nutrients. The farmer only
has to cultivate a few times, because once the cornstalks get going,
*they* take away the essentials from the weeds. The old weeds cannot
take over again, and the desirable, healthy plants no longer need
any help.

This analogy helps clients replace old, bad habits with new, good
ones. Of course, discouragement can stop them if they notice bad
habits reappearing after they have decided to turn over a new leaf.
Suppose they adopt new "cultivated" habits in their actions and
thought life, but then slip back into the old ways that they hoped
they had removed forever? It is here I reassure them that they
simply need to remove the weeds of their old habits by confessing
and repenting *every time they appear.* Their new habits will eventually grow to the point where they crowd out the old. Just like the
farmer who cultivates his seedlings, they fight a *winning* battle
against old habits by continuing to feed and exercise their new
growth.

### 9. The Other End of the Tongs:

When undergoing painful circumstances, people often ask,
"Where is God when it hurts?" I sometimes answer, "At the other
end of the tongs." I go on to explain that, even if God does not
arrange the agonizing circumstances that bombard us, he is too
economical to waste them. So, when we undergo a fiery ordeal of

grief or disappointment, he positions us *within* the fire, as would a blacksmith forging a valuable tool. God intends always to turn all our circumstances to the service of his long-term purpose: that we shall "participate in the divine nature" (2 Peter 1:4).

Yet, we feel the fire and think ourselves abandoned there. But notice the heat—it gives proof of the Master Craftsman at the other end of the tongs, shaping us for his purposes—"For we are God's workmanship . . ." (Eph. 2:10).

### 10. Second Murder:

Becky Pippert, well-known writer and speaker, tells about a woman who approached her after a speech. The woman said she could not get over a burden of guilt for an abortion she had years before. Although she had confessed it as sin, and by faith knew she had received God's forgiveness and cleansing, she did not *feel* relieved of her guilt.

· The woman said, "I killed someone and can't get over it. I just can't believe that I would do something that horrible." Becky paused, sensed God's guidance, then gently answered, "*I* can believe that you would do something that horrible. I can believe that you would commit that murder. I can believe it because it was not your first murder, but your second. You had already killed the lovely Son of God."

The woman dissolved into tears that this time *did* bring relief. She could now see herself as precisely the kind of person who needed a Savior. She could understand herself as "a sinner," and stop flattering herself as "a nice person" who happened to perform a sin uncharacteristic of an otherwise noble character. The evil we do does not contradict who we are, but reveals it.

Effective Christian counselors do not relieve guilt by minimizing wrongdoing, but by fostering full recognition of the deadliness of human sin. That Christ died for our sins means that, by sinning, we killed him. Our sin nature calls for a death penalty, but Jesus, the voluntary Substitute, offers the only remedy drastic enough to pay the penalty for us. We get relief only by welcoming his payment on our behalf. To do that, we must shamefacedly admit that we did nothing less than cost him his life—our first murder. Then we let his death achieve its purpose, by telling God we offer it as payment in full for *our* debt.

### 11. Nathan the Prophet:

Sometimes people ask me how they can confront someone else who persists in flagrant wrongdoing. The confronters face the tricky task of mentioning the wrong to someone who may not realize it and is likely to take offense when told.

I recommend that they follow the example of Nathan, the Old Testament prophet who confronted the adulterous killer, King David (2 Sam. 12). He approached the king with a story! In it, he appealed to David's excellent quality of compassion and his keen motivation for justice. I recommend that my inquirers find the counterparts in any person they must confront. The approach begins in a way that arouses and highlights fine qualities in the wrongdoer. Then it calls for that transgressor to apply those admirable traits to remedy his or her own wrongs.

Let's imagine an example. A church youth director goes to one of the leading laymen in the church to confront him about his harsh and aloof treatment of his own teenage son. The director says, "I have appreciated your years of dedicated service here as a fourth-grade Sunday-school teacher. The kids think highly of you because they know they matter to you. You go out of your way to show personal interest in them and to build them up. And I'm wondering, if I asked your teenage son if *he* feels important to you, what do you think he would say?" That message would probably get through!

## Using Compliments to Reframe

Since I take pains to give all my reframing a predominantly positive slant, throughout my conversations with clients I place the finest construction on their intentions, their characters, and their abilities. The Bible's description of love speaks clearly to this point: "Love . . . is ever ready to believe the best of every person" (1 Cor. 13:7, AMPLIFIED).

A hundred years ago, Henry Drummond went further with this verse in his analysis of 1 Corinthians 13, *The Greatest Thing in the World* (Drummond 1959, 37):

> Love thinketh no evil, imputes no motive, sees the bright side, puts the best construction on every action. What a delightful state of mind to live in! . . . For the respect of another is the first restoration

of the self-respect a man has lost; our ideal of what he is becomes to him the hope and pattern of what he may become.

Besides a general salting with compliments all through my counseling, I have recently begun using a formal complimenting procedure to close each appointment. I schedule sessions for forty-five minutes plus five minutes of closure. At forty minutes into a session, I excuse myself for about five minutes to go into another room and think over what we have talked about. I write out four or five things I genuinely admire about what the clients have said and how they have addressed their problems. I then re-enter the counseling room to deliver the results of my "think time." (For more on this tactic, see chapter 9.)

That five-minute break creates an extraordinary eagerness in clients to hear what I have to say in our closing moments. The break punctuates the session. It distills it down to these few summary remarks. Clients wait spellbound, as if for the results of an election, the verdict of a jury, or the conclusion of a suspense story. What I say after the break goes in with double or triple the impact of comments I make during the first forty minutes. Clients brace themselves to hear the worst, but they relax with appreciative relief when I speak the best. I deliver my compliments, offer a recommendation or "homework assignment," and set the next appointment, if any. Here follow some examples of compliments:

I was impressed by your determination to make things better. You showed courage in setting up this counseling appointment. You have made excellent use of your time here. And it's obvious that you really care what happens.

I was struck by your conscientious dedication to thoroughness in what you do. (That has a much more healing effect than if I said, You're too much of a perfectionist. Relax!)

I was moved by your capacity to feel deeply (if the client cried during our session).

One thing that really came across to me was how exquisitely fine-tuned you are to your body and your emotions (to clients who fret about minor aches and pains or detail their physical and mental sensations).

I noticed what an alert observer you are of the things that go on between you and your husband. (This one I might give at the end of my second session with a wife whom I had urged in our first session to observe in detail how her fights with her husband start, progress, and conclude.)

Most people feel a closure hunger at the end of a session. This formal feedback process takes care of it and also elevates my trustworthiness in their eyes. They respect me more as an expert who offers them a considered assessment of their condition. When I don't provide this kind of closure, clients often grope for it with questions like, "Are we getting anywhere? Are you sure you can help me? How long will I have to keep coming?"

Reframing helps clients to think their thoughts from a refreshingly different slant. But sometimes they don't think at all about taking certain bold actions that may resolve their problems. They consider such courage "unthinkable." As counselors we help them to think the unthinkable.

# 4

# Think the Unthinkable

Unemployed and supported by his wife, twenty-six-year-old Archie came to counseling, saying he wanted to get his act together in terms of a job.

*Counselor:* So you want to get and keep a job that uses and rewards your talents.
*Archie:* Right.
*Counselor:* What ways have you thought of to find a job?
*Archie:* Oh, the want ads in the paper.
*Counselor:* Do you have any objection to finding a job from the want ads?
*Archie:* No, I guess not.
*Counselor:* Have you called to inquire in the past week about any jobs listed in the want ads?
*Archie:* No.
*Counselor:* What do you think would happen if you did?
*Archie:* They might turn me down.
*Counselor: Then* what would happen?
*Archie:* I would be right back where I started.
*Counselor:* How would that be a problem for you?
*Archie:* I would feel like a failure.
*Counselor:* You mean you do not keep on calling until you get a job?
*Archie:* Oh, I could never do that!
*Counselor:* What do you think would happen if you did?
*Archie:* I would just be rejected over and over again.
*Counselor:* How many rejections do you think you might need to tolerate before you get an acceptance?
*Archie:* I don't know—fifteen, maybe twenty.
*Counselor:* Does getting a job matter enough to you that you might simply decide it's worth the price of twenty disappointments?
*Archie:* All I know is, I can't stand rejection.
*Counselor:* So a job is *not* worth twenty rejections to you.
*Archie:* I guess not.
*Counselor:* On the other hand, what does it cost you to *not* have a job?
*Archie:* It really hurts my self-esteem. I feel inferior to my wife, and she gets disgusted with me. I don't have the money to do the things I'd like. And I feel embarrassed when people ask me what I do for a living.

*Counselor:* I'm astonished at the mountain of disappointment you have been willing to endure up until now, to spare yourself twenty molehill disappointments.

*Archie:* They're not molehills, I tell you. I can't *stand* rejection.

*Counselor:* Are you sure?

*Archie:* What do you mean?

*Counselor:* Well, I understand you don't *like* rejection. Nobody does, of course, and maybe you hate it even more intensely than most people. But when you say you *can't* stand it, I'm puzzled. If you truly lack the ability to survive rejections, then I don't see how you can be here alive today talking to me about it, because you had to have undergone some in order to know that you don't like them. That's why I ask, are you sure you absolutely *cannot* endure job turndowns?

*Archie:* Hmm, all I know is I dread it so much that I just can't force myself to go ahead and make the calls.

*Counselor:* Archie, I have a vision for you. I see that dread like a wall standing between you and your future fulfillment in a job. And, in this vision, I see you symbolized by several different animals, each one representing a talent in your makeup. Each has a way to get past the barrier. One is a beaver with diamond teeth that can even chew through concrete. Another is a bird that flies over it. Then there's a speedy cheetah that can run around either side of it. And some kind of burrowing critter quickly digs a tunnel under the wall and comes out the other side to sign that employment contract. Knowing yourself, which one do you think probably gets there first?

*Archie:* I'm not sure. It's not that easy, you know.

*Counselor:* Hmm, that's a good point. You know, on second thought, this phone calling may not be such a hot way to get a job. You might already be doing the smartest thing to land a job that really fits you. I mean, holding back and waiting for them to come to you is a good way to be sure that they really *want* you.

*Archie:* Man, hearing you say it, it sounds really stupid. But that's what I've been doing—waiting for them to come to me. They're not gonna do that. I'd have to wait a thousand years. I've got to be the one to make the call if I want the job.

*Counselor:* I don't know, Archie. It's not good to be too hasty about things as important as this.

*Archie:* Hasty! Why, I haven't been hasty enough. I'm sick of sitting around waiting. I'm going to get a newspaper and go straight home to make those calls·til I get a job—today! See you later.

THE CONCEPT. The problems that people bring to counselors often consist of "blocks"—that is, reluctance to take some appropriate, effective action to accomplish a goal. Scripture urges boldness as a godly character trait when it says "Fear not!" Psychologists teach assertiveness to overcome anxiety. "Thinking the unthinkable" addresses block and boldness in vitality therapy.

The above illustration shows Archie's male counselor following a cogent sequence of steps that will be explained in later sections of this chapter:

1. He hears the problem, as shown by his summary statement: "So you want to get and keep a job that uses and rewards your talents."
2. He prescribes direct action: "Have you called to inquire in the past week about any jobs listed in the want ads?"
3. He asks the key question that prompts Archie to think the unthinkable: "What do you think would happen if you did?"
4. He asks it again: "*Then* what would happen?"
5. He persists in pushing Archie's thinking into the unthinkable, throughout the procedure, with such questions as: "How would that be a problem for you?"/"Are you sure?"/"How many rejections do you think you might need to tolerate before you get an acceptance?" (This last question also prescribes the healthy attitude of tolerating frustration.)
6. He establishes an impasse, clarifying Archie's refusal: "So a job is *not* worth twenty rejections to you."
7. He does *not* (in this example) try to resolve the impasse by pushing through with some command like, "Archie, just do it." But this simple step often does work well.
8. He counts the cost of Archie's inaction: "On the other hand, what does it cost you to *not* have a job?"
9. He shows astonishment several times, especially with an incredulous tone of voice: "You mean you do not keep on calling until you get a job?"/"I'm astonished at the mountain of disappointment you have chosen to endure up until now, to spare yourself twenty molehill disappointments."
10. He indirectly verbalizes Archie's hidden beliefs more or less as follows (speaking as Archie): "I lack the ability to survive rejections. I know this is true because I have been rejected several times and as you can see, I *am* dead."
11. He uses imagination and role-play: "Archie, I have a vision. . . ."

12. He finishes with psycho-judo (the reverse psychology of paradoxical or devil's-advocate tactics): "Hmm, that's a good point. . . . It's not good to be too hasty. . . ."

## The Key Question

Before we look in detail at each of the steps of "thinking the unthinkable," let's focus on the most useful single element of the whole procedure—the key question.

### Why It Works

"What do you think would happen if you did?" Most people have simply not thought to answer that important question when they fearfully rule out some sort of suitable action (call it X) to solve a problem. They have made action X unthinkable by an incomplete inner process in which they concluded that X was out of the question. But, when *you* ask, "What might happen if you did X?" you bring the matter back into serious consideration.

Your sheer act of asking implies two things: (1) your belief that doing X will probably bring about the positive result that the person wants; and (2) your vote of confidence in the person's ability to handle any negative results of doing X. You can, of course, come right out and say those two things *after* the person answers your question. Typically a client talks about only the negative results that X might bring, and you can challenge that in one of the following ways:

"Besides those difficulties you *don't* want, do you suppose that doing X will also produce the result you *do* want?"

"You make it sound as if the *only* outcome will be these negative results."

"And what else might happen?"

"I think you can handle that."

"Well, maybe it's worth it."

### Variations

You can present the key question in several different ways. For example, asking "What's the *worst* thing that might happen if you do X?" often quickly leads people to see their fears as absurd.

Sometimes what they fear has the most miniscule probability of occurring. That could apply to such grandiose beliefs as: "If I make a mistake, *everyone* will reject me." At other times "the worst thing" sounds tame when put into words. Example: "If I leave the house after checking all the lights only once, I might come home four hours later to discover I left one on by accident." To which you might respond, "Let's see, a hundred-watt bulb for four hours at seven cents per kilowatt hour will cost you about three cents."

When people tell you the worst thing that might happen, you can emphasize their capability with responses like these:

"Could you live with that?"

"What about deciding you're willing to endure that?"

"How would that be a problem for you?"

(Laughingly) "You make it sound like you don't think you can handle that!"

"Hmm, I suppose that could happen. And it certainly would not be pleasant if it did. But do you know what? I have a hunch that if anyone can handle that, *you* can."

"Okay, let's suppose the worst *did* happen. Besides what you *don't* like about it, what would there also be that you *could* like? What might be some benefits along with the negatives?"

You might increase the impact of the key question by asking, "What *will* happen *when* you do X?" "Will" and "when" convey future certainty, compared to the tentative and conditional "would" and "if." You perform a helpful verbal sleight-of-hand when you turn the focus away from *whether* a person will do X. When you focus instead on the results he or she will face, you presuppose that the person *is* going to do it. By answering your question, a client is unobtrusively buying into your presupposition and beginning to examine future circumstances, which include as an accomplished reality their having done X.

Consider also the subtle difference between these two wordings: (1) "What might happen if you do X?" and (2) "What *do you think* might happen if you do X?" The second opens the person's *thinking* for examination. It implies gently, "You could be wrong in your prediction."

Alternatively you might ask, "What do you *fear* might happen if you do X?" That steers directly into the emotional aspect of the person's hesitation, which generally ends up as the focus anyway. You can ask it that way when the primary help you intend to offer consists of reducing the person's anxiety. Usually, however, I prefer to ask people what they *think* might happen. It holds open the possibility for the person to answer that something good will happen.

"What keeps you from doing X?" This form of the key question leads well into visualization, using imagination and role-play techniques to resolve blocks. If people answer that fear holds them back, you can ask them to imagine fear as if it were a giant hand holding them by some sort of leash. Then you can create with them a miniature drama or mental movie in which they cut the cord or (if appropriate) invite Jesus in to pry open that cruel hand. A sophisticated professional therapist here could guide them into exploratory dialogue with the giant behind the hand. This generally evolves into a tearful reconciliation with some powerful person in their past, whose hardness they now come to see was motivated by fears, insecurity, and inferiority feelings. The solvent of compassion dissolves more anxiety than the sword of hostility slays.

### Pursuing It

If asking the key question catches half the people off guard, asking it a second time surprises 90 percent. For example, a shy man we'll call Don tells me that he just cashed a check at a local bank and received large bills, although he much prefers small ones.

I ask, "What do you think would have happened if you had asked for small bills?"

Don answers, "The teller would have been mad at me."

I pursue: "What do you think would have happened if the teller got mad at you?"

Don's mouth drops open, he blinks at me in bewilderment, hesitates for several seconds, then stammers out, "Why, I don't know. I never thought that far ahead."

Don took for granted that having a teller angry at him was so catastrophic that he must avoid it at all cost. On top of that, he had years of experience with other people reinforcing that belief. Some of his friends argued that people would not be mad at him for making small demands on them. Others agreed that, for a shy, sensitive guy like Don, a teller's anger would be devastating. My question pursued the matter by inviting Don a step beyond where he had always stopped.

Here are several different ways that you can question the fearful answer that someone gives to your first key question:

"What would be the awful thing about that?"

"Then what?"

"What would happen next?"

"How would that be a problem for you?"

"How would you probably handle it if that did happen?"

"Then what could you do?"

### When They Say, "I Don't Know"

In answer to your question, "What do you think would happen if you did X?" people often say they "have no idea." Generally you can get them to venture an answer by nudging them a little:

"What do you think?"

"Guess."

"Make it up."

"What *could* happen?"

"What would you say if you did know?"

"Think a minute" (then wait fifteen or twenty seconds).

As another tactic, you might ask, "How can you find out?" This remark urges an experimental attitude. After all, X represents an action likely to bring the desired result, yet the person refuses to do it, without knowing why.

## Steps to Produce Action

Now let's consider a full, formal procedure you can use to budge people past blocks in their lives.

1. *Hear the problem.* Listen specifically for people to describe their problems in terms that *could* be solved by bold action, if only they would do it. Restate in your own words your understanding of

the block as the other person sees it. (Use paraphrasing skills presented in chapter 1.)

For example, a shy employee complains to you about not getting a raise but is too scared to ask the boss for one. You verbalize the block: "So you hesitate to ask for the raise you feel you have earned." By this extra step, in which you clarify your understanding of the person's block, you follow the sound advice in Proverbs 18:13: "He who answers before listening—that is his folly and his shame."

2. *Prescribe direct action.* Think of how *you* would solve the problem in the most direct, healthy way. Then consider your clients "innocent until proven guilty." Assume they have simply not thought of taking straightforward action and that they will surely do so as soon as it occurs to them. Any hesitation therefore represents an oddity toward which you will direct fascinated attention, as in solving a puzzle.

In practice, maybe 5 percent of the people you counsel never thought of taking action X, and another 20 percent dismissed it too quickly when they thought of it. Taken together, these 25 percent may find your boost all they need to proceed with X. Probably the other three-quarters of your clients hold a catastrophic expectation that biases them against doing X. All told, therapeutically you can't lose when you prescribe action X. Either you help people past a block, or you bring to light an underlying fear that keeps *several* blocks in place.

For example, suppose you help a shy woman resolve the fear that keeps her from asking a waiter to take her undercooked entrée back to the kitchen. Then later, on her own, she may speak up to a supervisor about someone who sexually harasses her on the job.

If X represents the direct action that most reasonable persons would take to resolve the problem at hand, propose it to your listener in one of the following ways:

"Have you tried X?"

"Have you considered doing X?"

"What about X?"

"Do X."

Avoid even implying, "I *want* you to do X." That turns the issue into a personal one between them and you, in which they will either please or disappoint you. If they start to think *you* need to have them get over this problem, they will feel obligated rather than motivated to do X.

In response to your direct suggestion, a few people will decide to do X. They will say that they never thought of it before, or that the fact you recommend it is all the boost they need. However, most will object and say they "can't" do X. They have banished X to the land of the unthinkable.

3. *Ask the key question*. As noted previously, here lies the heart of this sequence of steps. When you ask, "What do you think would happen if you did X?" you directly invite people to "think the unthinkable." You nudge them to bring that old yet possible solution out of the mental mothballs in which they have stored it for years.

Occasionally you need go no further in the sequence. In thinking about what might happen if they do X, some people decide that it will solve their problem. Then, in doing a quick cost analysis, they conclude that, by comparison to that benefit, the likely difficulties they will face are minor inconveniences.

If people answer the key question with some catastrophic prediction, restrain yourself from arguing that what they fear will *not* happen. Instead, disagree with their self-appraisal of their inability to handle it. Minimize the severity of the outcome in relation to the capability of the person who suffers it.

4. *Ask it again*. Most people will tell you about some unbearably painful result they fear if they do X. You can pursue your question by continuing to ask, "What will happen next?" or "Then what?" This line of questioning works well when people describe tangible events they predict will be brought on by X.

For example, let's say direct action X calls for a shy wife to tell her thoughtless husband that she would like him to take more time to arouse her in their sexual foreplay. Hearing that suggestion, she objects, "He will get mad at me." You ask, "Then what?"

The woman looks at you surprised, as if she never imagined that life could continue beyond her husband's anger. She answers, "Well, I think he would quit lovemaking." The dialogue might continue as follows:

You ask, amazed, "Forever?"

She says, "No, just that time."

You ask, "Then what?"

She answers, "He would just roll over and not talk to me."

You ask, "And then what?"

She answers, "Well, he would still be mad in the morning."

You ask, "Then what?"

She answers, "I guess he would eventually talk to me."

You ask, "And then?"

She answers, "Well, I don't know. I never thought that far."

Sometimes, instead of asking what will happen next, you may prefer to ask, "What would be the awful thing about that for you?" This works particularly well when people answer the key question in terms of an inner emotional reaction. For example, the above woman hesitates to tell her husband that she would like him to build her up more before he seeks his own climax. She says that she would feel terrible for being too demanding.

You ask, "What would be the terrible part about being demanding?"

She says, "I would be unlovable."

You ask, "What would be the horrible thing about being unlovable?"

She answers, "I would be rejected, abandoned, utterly alone, and
unwanted."

Then you apologize for asking again, since it apparently seems to her that anyone with an ounce of sense would consider *that* answer the ultimate, unsurpassable horror. But you persist: "For-give me if I seem a little dense or unsympathetic or something, but I really want to know, what would be the awful, terrible, horrible, excruciating thing about it *for you* if you were unwanted?"

Now she has to think specifically what she does not like about what she fears. Every second she spends thinking this way moves the possibility out of the realm of the unthinkable. She begins to see that the matter boils down to one of *preference*. When you press her to the end, her final answer becomes, "Well, I just don't *like* it, that's all."

In response, you can say, "Exactly!" or "Right!" or "Of course!" or "Bingo!" You might add, "It really is a choice, isn't it?" Then you can follow up by asking what it would free her to do if she decided to tolerate having her husband mad at her, even though she doesn't like it. In all of this process, you are working to decrease her hatred of the outcome she does not like, and to increase her attraction to the successful portion she does like.

You also create another effect when you exaggerate by asking what would be the "awful, terrible, horrible, excruciating thing" about the husband's angry rejection. You throw her fears into the realm of absurdity and thus imply that she does not have to regard her husband's anger as intolerable.

5. *Persist.* You seek in all of your pursuit to arouse doubt in a client's mind about the inevitability of the feared outcome and about the person's unexamined belief that he or she does not have what it takes to survive it. You lead in the direction of having the person consider taking the unpleasant consequence in stride. Here are some questions you can ask to increase this healthy doubt:

"Are you sure you couldn't handle it?"

"What are the chances that this result will occur?"

"How many people do you know who have ever died from that consequence?"

With a person who insists, "I can't do X," ask, "Do you wish you could?"

A teasing challenge often works well when the feared consequence falls into the category of looking foolish, feeling embarrassed, or being laughed at. You can further lampoon these inflated fears by joking, "I can see it all now—a newspaper headline: 'Woman Brazenly Challenges Husband.' And below that: 'Pushy Wife Barred from Polite Society.'"When you get people to laugh at their own exaggerated thinking, you put them into an objective position of observing themselves. Laughter comes from a stance *outside* the situation.

Another example of pursuing the key question arises when you repeatedly ask people what they think will happen if they persist with action X as long as necessary to get a desired result. This sequence applies particularly to discouragement. For example, the woman above says that it would not work to tell her husband she wants him to spend more time and loving attention to arouse her. "He would just rush ahead anyway," she insists.

Then you ask, "And what will happen if you repeat your request a second time, more emphatically, like, 'Honey, honey! Slow down! Come on, bring me along with you!'?"

She answers, "I could never do that."

You pursue, "What would happen if you did?"

She answers, "It still would not work."

Then you ask, "And suppose you tell him a third time, even more vigorously, 'John, I really mean it. I *want* to be in this with you. Please take time to include me'?"

Notice that, within your questions, you are also demonstrating for her how she could address her husband. When X is embedded within your questions, the idea sticks in her mind better than it would in the form of direct advice. You are modeling for this shy woman some bold, assertive actions that she has probably never seriously considered.

Suppose she says, "He would still go ahead, ignoring me."

You pursue, "Then the fourth time you make it even *more* clear: 'John, I feel as if you're not paying attention to what I'm telling you. Our lovemaking really matters to me. And when you don't even respond to what I'm saying, I feel less included than ever. What do you hear me saying, John?' Of course, by this time, you are sitting up in bed, looking him in the eyes. I mean that your words and actions go together. So what do you predict will happen *then*?"

In this line of pursuit, you attack a different issue in this woman's life than just confronting her husband. You focus on her insufficient persistence. Later you connect the two by pondering aloud, "I wonder if, by persisting, you might reassure your husband that you are not merely tolerating him, but that you definitely want an emotional involvement with him. But how can he know unless you put *your* emotions into the requests you make of him?"

6. *Establish an impasse.* When you keep asking pursuit questions, you create a progression of answers, nested within each other. For example:

> "The awful thing if I do X is that I might look foolish."
>
> "The awful thing about looking foolish is that people would not like me."
>
> "The awful thing about people not liking me is that I would forever more be an outcast."

"The awful thing about being an outcast is that I would feel so lonely I would not want to live anymore."

"And the awful thing about that is . . . well, I cannot imagine anything worse than that."

At that point you have reached the most rock-bottom horror that the person can imagine. This ultimate unthinkable almost always reflects some aspect of rejection or abandonment. No wonder that Scripture portrays hell as outer darkness—that utterly forsaken loneliness that we all fear as "the fate worse than death."

At this point of impasse, you make the connection clearly in words: "So you refuse to do X because you are sure that it cannot help but lead directly to your being utterly abandoned forever by everyone." This inflated statement often prompts people to laugh and qualify it. They reflect, "Well, when you say it that way, it sounds pretty silly." You might immediately pick up on that by asking, "What's silly about it?" If you can redirect them into arguing against their own mistaken belief, the sequence may have served its purpose.

## Resolving an Impasse

But let us suppose that a person has gone as far as the ultimate unthinkable with you and has *agreed* to your inflated summary statement. Now the two of you have really come to an impasse! How can you proceed?

### Push Through

Especially when you have a good relationship with the person you are counseling, you can sometimes simply direct him or her to move through the emotional barrier by saying things like:

"Come on. You can do it. I know you have what it takes."

"Do it anyway."

"I believe in you."

"You'll be setting a good example for others."

"This is exactly the kind of practice you need in building boldness."

"I'll give you a dollar."

"I *dare* you!"

"Do it *because* you don't want to."

"What will it take to get you to do this?"

"*Risk* it!"

"Have you considered living with the pain as a price worth paying to get the result you're after?"

"I want to suggest something to you. Okay? *Just accept the pain.* I mean it. Think the unthinkable! Decide to tolerate what you have until now considered *in*-tolerable."

"Look, if this idea does not work, I need to know exactly what happens when you try it. Because then I can help you figure out a different way that has a better chance of working. But right now I need you to do your part."

Sometimes you can induce people to do X as an experiment, to see (1) whether the horror they predict actually does occur; and (2) just how catastrophic that outcome is, compared to their ability to escape, endure, or overcome it. You might suggest that they try a small, watered-down portion of X. You thus show that you stand on the side of their safety and do not expect them to heroically solve all their fears at once. By respecting their fears, you free people from having to convince you that things are worse than you realize.

To go further in this direction, you can reassure people that they still have their old avoidance techniques available as a refuge. They do not have to give them up in order to add new, bolder techniques to their repertoire. By talking "experiment," you frame X as worth doing for the information value, whether or not it accomplishes the final result it aims at. This approach appeals particularly to psychology-minded persons who want to learn more about the nature of anxiety and coping techniques. You can reframe their circumstances as a "laboratory," in which "experience is the best teacher." You might even arouse this interest by asking if they have ever wanted to study psychology. (Most people will say yes to that. Introductory Psychology generally ranks as the most popular course on college campuses!)

Particularly if you will have no future opportunity with a person, or if your own time is at a premium, you can just lay it on the line. You might say, "If you do not cooperate by at least trying, I cannot help you and there will really be no point in our talking further. I need some evidence that you take my counsel seriously."

### Count the Cost

So far, in clarifying the impasse, you have emphasized the cost that people anticipate from *doing* X. Now you flip the coin over and ask what it costs them *not* to do X. You perform a cost-benefit analysis of their hesitation. You minimize the benefit as being merely security. Then you list all the prices they pay by not acting:

The problem continues.

They stay frustrated.

They sacrifice satisfaction.

They think poorly of themselves.

They sacrifice the chance to learn a new skill.

They settle for the status quo.

Further tip the balance by citing a long list of the benefits that could come from doing X. Then point out that the person you are counseling chooses to give up all that by refusing to do X. You can approach this procedure another way, too: "We've talked a lot about what you would *not* like about doing X. But what's the other side of it? What can you find to actually *like* about it?"

You may try another tactic: "Suppose you made a firm decision *not* to do X, *ever,* and to go through life without its benefits. What would you miss about it if you knew you were never going to have the outcome you long for?" (I will say more later in this book about how to use the paradoxical techniques of playing devil's-advocate.)

To get people to feel the weight of their decisions as heavily as possible, try proposing this: "Now look me in the eyes and say with a straight face, 'I refuse to ever do X no matter what it costs me.'" Since people typically refuse to be that blunt about their decisions, you can sometimes simply let that go unchallenged as a seed of doubt about their refusal. Other times you might probe into why they hesitate to utterly rule out doing X: "Sounds like you have *some* interest in doing X. What do you make of that?"

### Show Astonishment

You can add to the pressure of counting the cost by making statements that further emphasize the personal price and therefore the oddity of the person's hesitation.

"I'm astonished at the high personal price you are willing to pay."

"What a staggering loss you are willing to sustain!"

"It's incredible that you are more dedicated to emotional safety than to emotional *and* mental *and* spiritual growth."

"I'm amazed. . . ."

"How unusual. . . ."

This may sound like putting a guilt trip on the person. However, these sentences do not condemn people as if they had let someone else down, but highlight the cost to themselves of their passivity. Perhaps Esau would not have given up his birthright for a mere portion of lentil stew if a friend had appeared on the scene and expressed therapeutic astonishment.

All the way along, I seek to arouse doubt in a sufferer's mind about the inevitability and seriousness of the outcomes he or she fears. I flavor my voice tone with astonishment. For example, a man hesitates to do X because "someone might yell." I try to clarify my understanding of his viewpoint by asking, "So you think it would be *awful* if someone yelled at you?" I make myself genuinely surprised as I do this, by holding in my mind's eye an image of this man as seven feet tall, muscular, and powerful. That mental picture accurately symbolizes my *chosen* belief in his capability.

### Verbalize Hidden Beliefs

In the example at the start of this chapter, the therapist asked Archie what he thought would happen if he kept calling for job interviews even after he got one or two turn-downs. Archie answered, "Oh, I could never do that." That exclamation rests on several unexamined beliefs by which Archie has put persistence into the "unthinkable" category. As counselor, you can get good at detecting the hidden beliefs that must lie behind that kind of refusal. A few examples appear in the following imaginary dialogue between Archie and counselor:

*Archie:* Oh, I could never do that!

*Counselor:* In other words, would you say it's an utterly impossible task that *nobody* could carry out?

*Archie:* Hmm, no, I'm sure that other people could do it, but *I* couldn't.

*Counselor:* In other words, you're different somehow.

*Archie:* Well . . . I . . . uh . . . I'm just not as capable in that area as other people.

*Counselor:* Would you say you've lost an ability you once had?

*Archie:* No, I've *never* been able to do anything like this.

*Counselor:* So, it's an area where you're kind of untrained, or underdeveloped? Like you grew up in a sort of overprotected privileged class? I mean weak, or fragile or flabby—something like that?

*Archie:* Well, that sounds kind of insulting when you say it that way.

*Counselor:* I don't mean to insult you. I only want to understand. Do you think you're too fragile to persist through several disappointments?

*Archie:* All I know is I just can't stand to be rejected.

*Counselor:* Well, would you say that these telephone job rejections will be delivered more harshly and frequently to *you* than to an ordinary person? Does life sort of conspire against you to give you a tougher time than the average guy?

*Archie:* Now come on, you're making me sound like I'm paranoid or something.

*Counselor:* Well, what about it? Do you think potential employers will give *you* a harder time than they give anyone else?

*Archie:* Well, no, probably not, but. . . .

*Counselor:* Would I be accurate in saying that the accumulated pain of twenty rejections *far* outweighs the satisfaction you will get from one acceptance?

*Archie:* Yes.

*Counselor:* And are you saying that you have *never* in your life before *ever* persisted toward a goal despite several setbacks, discouragements, or rejections?"

*Archie:* Well, I've never liked it.

*Counselor:* That sounds like you *have* done it. Like—did you ever try out for a Little League team, strike out a lot, but stick at it anyway?"

*Archie:* Well, sure, I did that.

*Counselor:* Now look me in the eyes and say with a straight face, "I was tougher when I was a kid."

That look-me-in-the-eyes intervention offers a good way to end the sequence of belief testing. Generally, people will just grin instead of actually doing what I ordered. And I do not press for compliance, since I know that I have made my point. The "straight face" phrase, of course, implies that I believe the opposite of the silent, hidden belief that I ask them to say out loud. In the above example, the counselor obviously considers Archie tougher now as a result of growing up in the school of hard knocks.

I might add an additional couple of comments, such as: "Then after that, keep a straight face while you say, 'If it were easier, I would do it.'" (That ought to tickle his "I'm not lazy" button.) Or, "Then give me the summary of the whole thing: 'I refuse to persist in asking for a job, no matter what my refusal costs me'."

In the above dialogue, each comment from the counselor puts into words a belief or policy that has to be true in order for Archie to say that he could never persist in calling for job interviews. But said bluntly, out loud and in the presence of another person, makes these beliefs far less acceptable to Archie than when he keeps them unverbalized, unexamined, and unquestioned in the shadows of his unconscious thinking. (Chapter 7 presents more on this powerful technique of challenging hidden beliefs.)

### Use Imagination and Role-Play

Since a picture is worth a thousand words, what people can *imagine* doing they can then plan and do. You want to get "stuck" people visualizing themselves "unstuck" in the future. This section considers a number of ways either to call forth or implant mental pictures of success.

Archie's counselor might ask, "If you do get yourself to persist in asking for jobs, how will you know when you are doing it?" The counselor can help Archie formulate a concrete answer such as, "When I have made at least three calls in one fifteen-minute period, regardless of the results."

The counselor could then ask for descriptions of sights and sounds: "How will the person on the other end let you know when you hit pay dirt? What will he or she say? Will you be invited to an interview? How will you dress for that? Who will probably be the first to mention salary?" Similarly, I sometimes ask people how their actions and the outcomes would look and sound on a videotape: "If all this were already completed and you and I were sitting here watching a video replay of it, how could I tell the difference between a successful call and one of your unsuccessful ones?"

I might ask Archie to visualize further: "In contrast to the discouraging times, how do you *wish* a call would go? Describe step-by-step for me a perfect call—your ideal dream—pure fairy-tale make-believe." I draw out his picture of a desirable outcome. I feed it with questions like these:

"How will you celebrate?"

"Who else will celebrate with you?"

"Who will you tell first?"

"How long will you have between the time you sign up and the time you start work?"

"How much on-the-job training will you probably need, and how well will your past experience probably equip you?"

"How far are you willing to drive every day to the job?" (This question has the added virtue of showing Archie that he *is* willing to pay *some* price to have a job. Even if he won't drive fifty miles, he may go five.)

You could also help to desensitize Archie's fears by living through them in imagination with him. So you ask, "Let's suppose that the first man you call does reject you. How will he probably do it? What will he say?" After Archie answers that, you persist: "What about the second guy? How might he reject you if he does it in a different way?" Then ask, "Now give me the worst one. Make up the most devastating possible rejection you can think of." Throw in some ideas of your own, like the guy snorting, "How dare you answer my ad!"

You could ask Archie some additional details: "Will you vary your style? Will you get extra polite sometimes, with 'Sir" and 'Ma'am?" This kind of quest for specifics of the process carries with it the presupposition that Archie *will* do the process. It accustoms him to actions that he has previously refused to consider. You make him more and more at home with the possibility, simply by discussion about it. This gentle, inquisitive process has far more effect than the nagging that Archie probably gets from loved ones—and fights off.

You might deliberately try to encourage a client with imagination. For example, "Archie, I want you to picture those rejections that are sure to come to you. See them as arrows shooting toward you. Here they come, closer and closer. But at the last instant they bounce off an invisible shield of godly courage that surrounds you." Or, in a different image, "See each rejection symbolized as a mosquito. They settle on your skin, but you swat them and brush them off before they have a chance to bite you. I mean, you recognize the early signals of your negative reaction to rejection. The first few vibes are like the mosquito's feet on your skin—kind of a tickle. At *that* moment, before you let discouragement develop, you swat it off by saying something like, 'I'm going on to the next one.' And you know that even if you wait a little too long and you do get bitten, it's only a mosquito bite on your skin, not a sword thrust through your heart." (Chapter 6 will present more in detail on the use of imagination in vitality therapy.)

*A personal application.* Some years ago, I failed to take an appropriate direct action and deeply regretted it afterward. I was teaching a Sunday-school class for fourth-graders. A parent kept me late after class one Sunday to talk about his child. This delayed me in picking up my own five-year-old son from another room. I finally got to him after all his classmates had left. I found him in considerable distress, thinking that his dad had forgotten him. I wish now that I had excused myself from the parent boldly yet pleasantly, in order to honor my first responsibility, to my own son.

When I analyzed why I did not assert myself in that way, I came up with this fear: "This man will not like me, and he will ruin my reputation." Since then I have speculated on how he might have smeared me if he decided to go to the trouble. He could have rented a sound truck to blare the message throughout several neighborhoods: "Dennis Gibson refused to talk to me. He is an unfit person. Join the Gibson Boycott Crusade and help stamp out a menace right here in River City." Maybe he would hire a blimp to trail a banner proclaiming "Impeach Gibson."

Even as I reread those exaggerated notions now, I get the same healthy reaction I did the first time I applied this therapy to myself. My dormant logic wakes up and says to my fears, "Come on, now, you're not *that* important." Making that discovery on my own does me far more good than hearing someone else reason with me, "That father would probably not ruin your reputation."

The fearful obsession that kept me from getting to my son on time rested on a foundation of vanity. I thought my boldness would trigger a massive investment of time and energy from the father. Confessing "I'm not *that* important" has created a counter-emotion of chagrin, which neutralized the fear that my grandiosity spawned.

### Use Psycho-Judo

A judo combatant tries to push his opponent over backward. He feels him resisting, so he quickly reverses his own effort and pulls *with* the direction his opponent is going. He uses his adversary's own momentum to throw him off balance, thus preventing a stale-mate between them.

Reverse psychology has recently enjoyed popularity under the heading of paradoxical techniques. Chapter 8 develops this theme further, but we will apply it here to resolve Archie's block against taking proper, persistent actions to get a job.

With Archie you could play a little bit of a devil's-advocate posi-tion by pondering aloud, "Maybe it's *not* worth it. Maybe the ordeal of rejection after rejection *is* too much price to pay compared to the tiny benefits of success. So let's imagine for a moment that you do persist, and it does work. What *further* kinds of hassles will you have to endure along with the new job?" You hope here, of course, that Archie will say that the joys of having a job outweigh any pressures that go with it and even the struggles to get it.

Reverse psychology is the native tongue of strong-willed adults. Others often see them as merely stubborn, but some folks just think in opposites. You speak their language when you say "black" to convey "white." When you shift into agreeing with their objec-tions, the only way they can continue to oppose you is to shift into defending *your* original position.

Archie says that he couldn't stand the rejections if he persisted in answering job ads. So you reflect soberly for a moment and then come out with some arguments that you truly *can* believe but that support his position: "You know, you may be right. The economy might not be quite healthy just now. Employers may be a little too belligerent these days. Nobody likes to be rejected. Maybe you ought to go easy for a while."

This line may tickle him into arguing, "I'm not sure that now is any worse time in the economy than any other time. And if I'm ever going to get a job, there's no time like the present."

At this point, do not agree with his new "enlightened" position.

If you were to say, "I knew you'd see it my way," he would just have to go back to his original opposition. Stay skeptical. Maintain mild pessimism: "Well, I hope you're not being rash."

Some people really rise to this bait. A challenge activates their vitality. They want to show you they're made of sterner stuff than you give them credit for.

# 5

# Grieve

Imagine that you are the pastor of a small church in a college town. Last year you enjoyed getting to know George, then a freshman. George has now returned for his sophomore year but is not doing well, and so comes to you for help.

George tells you that his father died suddenly the week after final exams the past spring. A heart attack took Dad's life while George was gone on a week-long canoe trip in a remote wilderness area. He returned in time for the funeral, but he blamed himself for not having been there when his father died.

George tells you that he thought he had wept through all his grief during the summer. It had not been easy, but he was over the symptoms of immediate grief. He has his appetite back and is sleeping normally again. However, he cannot regain his concentration for college studies. You need to help him over the debilitating effects of this heavy loss in his life. How can you make the most of an hour or two with George?

THE CONCEPT. The previous chapter focused on blocks motivated by the fear of taking bold action. Sometimes, however, the block that a client faces rests more on grief. Suffering some loss may have drained away from a person his or her motivation to move ahead in life. The unthinkable *has* happened, and the sufferer has trouble accepting it. This chapter will describe ways in which you can foster grieving to get people past the stuck points that result from heartache, thereby enabling them to get on with living.

## The Purpose of Grief

We can define any emotion as energy available to accomplish a task. *Joy* is energy to celebrate some favorable event. *Fear* is energy to flee danger. *Guilt* is energy to confess and repent a wrong. *Righteous anger* is energy to correct an injustice. *Sadness* is energy available to complete the hard work of letting go our attachment to something precious we have lost. It can be a person, place, position, or a possibility that has become out of our reach. Along with letting go, grieving calls for celebrating what was.

Recognize grief and joy as two sides of a coin, which symbolizes something we value. With joy we celebrate our involvement with a cherished object. With grief we declare our pain upon its removal from us. Certain problems that clients bring can be solved only by accepting a loss. Grieving gives us a solution when we cannot restore what we have lost. It helps us go on with our lives.

Death of a loved one represents the prototype loss. When an immediate family member or a close friend dies, the survivors suffer—and need to grieve for—the loss of that person's companionship. Gone, too, is the chance to share mutual memories from the past, as well as hopes and dreams for the future. For example, if a pregnancy ends tragically in a miscarriage, husband and wife lose more than just the life of their baby; they also lose, at least for a while, their dream of parenthood.

Broken relationships range from boyfriend-girlfriend break-up to divorce, which tears asunder a husband-wife one-flesh union. Such jolts in life give their victims a sense of helpless bereavement. Losing a job, failing to win at a contest we trained for strenuously, or getting bad news about our health can also jar and deprive us of a reason for joy. When a natural disaster occurs—a tornado, flood, or earthquake—people suffer "post-traumatic disorders." The stresses experienced in such sudden and violent dislocations of lives are best solved by the reliving and relieving inherent in the mourning process.

Sometimes we go into mourning over violations of our person. Being molested, raped, robbed—even if it happened years ago in childhood—steals from us the safety of our personal space.

Sometimes within our grief we also feel guilt or remorse over things we did wrong (or thought we did). For example, women who have had abortions often need help getting over both disabling emotions. As counselor in these situations especially, you become a priest who must witness and facilitate the healing rituals involved in confession and in grieving. This chapter will describe concrete steps you can take to enable people to move forward rather than remain mired in the unfinished business created by a loss in their lives.

## Encourage Tears

Tears usually mark the letting-go process. They even initiate and enable it to happen, as if they lubricate the friction associated with moving from one phase of life to another. Sobbing can relieve built-up stress and keep it from becoming *dis*-tress. Tears also connect the mourner with the whole human family of sobbing sufferers down through history. For these and other reasons, people who come to you for help after a loss should be encouraged to express their grief openly. One or more of the following techniques is often helpful:

1. *Ask for details*. See yourself again counseling George, the college sophomore who lost his dad. You could ask some of the following:

"How did it happen?"

"Tell me about your dad."

"What kind of a guy was he?"

"What would I have liked about him?"

"What did the two of you used to do together?"

2. *Give permission*. When George does cry, you can normalize it by saying things like, "This is *worth* crying about." Or, suppose George puts himself down with some remark like, "I should be over this by now." Ask him, "Why? Are you sure? Do you really think so?" Be a little amazed that he thinks he should not be crying. Add such reframes as:

"We can only be sad over the loss of things that matter a great deal to us."

"Your tears are a tribute to your father. They show how much he meant to you as a dad."

"Your tears certainly make *me* think highly of him."

In my office, I keep a box of Kleenex within easy reach of my clients. Generally, when they come to the verge of tears, they glance at the box. I comment simply, "Most people cry here."

I have seen some therapists fail at trying to encourage tears by saying direct things like, "Just let it come. Stay with that feeling. Go ahead and cry." These commands obligate people to cry, instead of letting them weep as a spontaneous outpouring. I get better results with statements like, "I can see that really moves you. Your feelings are certainly right there ready to come, aren't they?"

3. *Have them say the words.* Here follows a list you can have George say to go through the ritual of acknowledging Dad's death and his own bereavement:

"Dad is gone."

"I miss him."

"I wish he were here."

"But he's not."

"I can't change that."

"I am sad."

"It helps to say it to someone else."

"I am better off for having known him."

You can use the above format with various people and different sources of grief. People generally balk at one of these steps more than at another, but what they don't want to say reveals their stuck point. Asking them what statement they don't want to repeat may get them to say it. Or asking what they think will happen if they say it may plant the words so that they say them internally. Even that usually starts their tears. If they then allow themselves to utter the words aloud, they often trigger their own deeply therapeutic, chest-heaving sobs, such as they have not known since childhood. That brings the most profound relief in the shortest time.

## Elicit Repetition

One of the best ways we get over a loss is by repeating to ourselves almost like a broken record something like, "I can't believe he's gone." The sheer repetition seems to embed the fact of the loss into our consciousness, thereby helping us past the denial phase of reaction to loss.

With George, you might have him repeat several times, "Dad is gone." You may even ask him to express the same thought in his own words in three different ways. Among these three, George may stumble onto one that uniquely unlocks his emotions. For example, he may say your assigned words, "Dad is gone," without a ripple of emotion. But when he comes out with his own paraphrase, "Dad's not around anymore," it plunges him into the unfettered sobbing he needs.

George's particular situation overlays his sorrow with a sense of guilt for not having been present when his father died. He may need to repeat such words as: "If only I had been there." As a counselor you want to budge him off the unproductive dead-end street of self-blame into a more realistic repetition: "I *wish* I had been there." Thus you help him relabel his painful emotion more accurately as "regret" rather than "guilt." He committed no crime, but merely unintentionally missed an opportunity he now urgently wishes he could have seized.

You may need to challenge the grandiose thinking involved in George's self-blame. When he grinds out, "If only I had been there," have him add, ". . . I surely could have saved his life." Sometimes that abrupt kind of confrontation of an unstated and unrealistic belief shocks people into realizing the truth of their own limited powers and hence their limited responsibilities. Alternatively, you might ask George what he would have done if he *had* been there. This could lead smoothly into the unforgettable, healing role-play of a goodbye scene, as we shall see next.

## Role-Play Goodbye

As you interview George, asking him such things as what Dad was like, make sure you ask about their last time together. Draw out George on what they did and said, where they were, and especially their last words and gestures to each other. That was the only goodbye they had, and by enhancing its vividness in George's memory, you help him to find it an ample one. Then ask this key question for the healing process: "If you had known that this was going to be the last time you would see your dad alive, what would you have wanted to say to him?" Then later ask, "And what would Dad have said to you?"

George will probably answer for himself with sentences like, "I love you. You've been a good dad. Thanks. I'll miss you." When he answers for his father, you can supply him with any of these that he leaves out:

"I'm sorry I have to leave you."

"I'm proud of you, son."

"I wish I had spent more time with you."

"I'm glad for the things we did together."

"Even if I never showed it much, I want you to know I love you."

"You'll be a fine dad yourself some day."

"Be a man of God, my son."

After George has filled in all the lines for both his dad and himself in his hallowed little vignette, ask him what Dad's very last words to him would be. Then prompt, "And how do *you* finish?" If he has not yet done so, have him quote each one as saying the crucial ending word, "Goodbye." Mark an end to the vignette at that point. Say something like, "That was beautiful," or "Thanks for letting *me* in on that."

Don't analyze this farewell scene afterward unless George particularly wants to discuss it. Otherwise take it for granted that he said goodbye to his dad emotionally in that imaginary conversation. All that remains are some sweet reveries and perhaps some talk about the future:

"What have you picked for a major?"

"When do you expect to finish college? Then what?"

"You got a girlfriend?"

"What kind of things were you and Dad planning to do together? Do you think you might still go ahead and do them?"

### With Non-Grievers

Many people who bring problems to you will mention only incidentally some loss in their lives. They do not intend for you to focus on the loss, because they do not consider it connected to the currently disturbing issue. But something may tell you that they have some important unfinished business to resolve concerning that loss. To prove it, you gently ask, "Did you get a chance to say goodbye to _____?" (Of course, the blank can represent a person, a pet, a home, a town, a part of the person's body, a job, a school, a building demolished—whatever apparently held your client's heartstrings.) If the person answers *no,* then you proceed with a precious though hypothetical goodbye ceremony (as in the above case of George).

When people answer that they *did* have a farewell conversation with a now-departed loved one, draw out the details, showing a cherishing interest. While asking who said and did what, weave in some questions that add richness and impact. For example, "Did your dad look you in the eyes and say from his heart, 'Son, I'm proud of you'?" Ask what else the person wishes he or she (or the loved one) could have added to make a fully satisfying goodbye.

Some therapists use techniques from psychodrama or Gestalt therapy to orchestrate a literal enactment of a goodbye scene. They have the client sit in one chair, facing an empty chair that represents the lost object of love. They lead the farewell conversation as if it were actually happening right then and there. When clients get into such a simulation, they generally experience more realism and emotional benefit than in talking *about* saying goodbye. However, I find most people distracted by a kind of self-conscious stage fright when I move furniture around and set rules about how to do it. The kind of easy, "as if" conversation I illustrated above with George seems more natural and less intrusive.

### Applying Forgiveness

`Goodbye scenes afford a good place to include some forgiveness dialogue. Perhaps the deceased loved one had directly offended your client by physical or sexual abuse, or had been aloof or alcoholic or mean to another family member. Or maybe your client had wronged the loved one and never confessed until now a harbored bitterness, an attitude of ingratitude, some petty thievery, or a sharp tongue. You can draw out these memories with questions like:

"Is there anything Dad would ask you to forgive him for?"

"Would you need to confess anything to him?"

"Would there be any remaining hurt that either of you would want to see healed and forgiven?"

You can, of course, use this forgiveness dialogue in a role-play scenario with a loved one who had not died, but who is estranged and not present. Wrongs that cannot be righted can be healed only by forgiveness, which is a process closely akin to grieving. For example, an incestuous brother cannot give back to his younger sister the virginity he stole from her. And he may never agree to meet with her and a counselor to ask her forgiveness. But she can release the burden within her own soul by practicing with your help the forgiveness conversation she *would* have if he ever did come penitently before her.

In many forgiveness cases, the client's bitterness gets in the way. For example, the woman above, whose brother molested her long ago, may have trouble imagining his apologizing to her. You speak for him by asking, "How would you answer if he said, 'I was wrong. I mistreated you. I thought only of myself and ignored your feelings.'?"

She protests, "He would never speak that way!"

You persist, "Maybe not, but *if* he did, how would you answer?"

She resists further: "I just can't see him ever admitting that he could be wrong."

You persist, "You're probably right, but that's not the most important part. You need to know *your* lines, not his. It's what *you* say that releases you from what *he* did. So how *would* you express your forgiveness if you were going to?"

### Grieving and Abortion

Women often suffer the double agonies of sorrow and guilt for having arranged a medical abortion to end a pregnancy they did not want. Later, when they consider that what they did was a violation of God's holy law against murder—and seek your help to find forgiveness and relief from their burden—you might find the following kind of scenario a powerful and moving experience for both of you:

> Start by telling the woman, "Imagine yourself standing trial in a courtroom in heaven. God the Father is there. So is Jesus. Dozens of angels are gathered around. God starts the proceedings by solemnly calling for the star witness, your unborn child." (Here you can ask the woman if she thinks of her dead child as a boy or girl, and then use that gender from here on.)
>
> "God speaks to your child and says, 'Here stands the woman I selected to give birth to you, raise you, protect you, and teach you about me. Instead, she rejected my assignment and had you put to death. Now tell me your verdict. What shall I do with her?'
>
> "Your child looks sadly at you, then turns to God and says, 'Father, forgive her. She did not know what she was doing.'
>
> "At this point, Jesus steps forward, bends down and takes your child on his lap. He looks you in the eyes and says, 'What you did to this little one of mine, you did to me. You deserve the death penalty for your sins but I have died in your place. Accept my sacrifice for you. Your child has not condemned you, and neither do I. Go, and do not repeat this great sin.'

"Then God permits you and your child to approach each other and speak. Oh, how you have longed for such a moment! What do you want to say and do?"

Next you help the woman to verbalize a wholehearted confession and repentance, including the words, "I was wrong." It should also include her statement of what she would do differently if she could go back to her choice point in the pregnancy.

Fill in the parts the child should say in a godly forgiveness. Keep it brief, such as, "I forgive you, Mom." You are not trying to assist the woman to make contact with the spirit of her departed child, but to experience the emotional effects of a biblical confession, repentance, forgiveness, and cleansing renewal. Finish the mother-child scene with "Goodbye" both ways. Then continue:

"Next, Jesus comes up to you to establish your new, forgiven identity in him, and to cleanse you from all stains. He takes you to a nearby body of water, wades in with you, and baptizes you. In fact, he submerges himself completely under the water with you. Then he pulls you up with him and explains, 'You have now been buried with me by this baptism into the death of your old self. And I have raised you to new life with me—my life in you!' At this Jesus embraces you, like a proud groom hugging his new bride at the wedding altar. And the place erupts with cheers and applause."

## Ask About the Future

"Christmas won't be the same without Dad, will it?" As George's counselor, you might ask this question for two reasons. First, it extends your main purpose, which is to prompt George to talk out how his life is different now, without Dad. Second, you help George to prepare for the inevitable restimulation of sadness he will feel at family times that once included his father.

By talking about those future times in counseling, you extend healing into those predictable events. When he actually comes to those poignant times, George will remember, "I've been here before. We talked about this in the pastor's office." This recollection will offset an unhealthy tendency for George to think during future sad times that he is not really over his dad's death and thus conclude, "I shouldn't feel sad now if I finished grieving. So this means I'm unstable." Talking about these feelings ahead of time normalizes future episodes of grief when they come.

When completed, the primary grieving period orients the be-reaved person to life without the lost love object. To that end, you might ask George, "How will the rest of your life benefit from having had precisely the father you had?" Besides getting George to talk more about his dad's fine qualities, you get him focusing on his own life without Dad. What you are really asking is: "How are you already a better person for having undergone this wrenching, heartbreaking loss of a father you loved very much?"

## Comments on Using Imaginative Techniques

Because of recent cautions expressed by Christian writers who fault the field of psychology (e.g., Hunt and McMahon 1985), I want to clarify the nature of the role-play conversations I have described in this chapter. I do not conjure up spirits of dead loved ones to encounter my clients or guide them. That would be an occult prac-tice, such as is used in seances. I described here how George was asked to think about what Dad would have wanted to say to him if he had had the chance before dying. I do not propose that the counselor ask what Dad *is* saying to George, as if he were present in some sort of visitation. Nor in the abortion forgiveness do I imply that mother and child actually make contact in my office. We pretend, in order to see with our heart's eyes.

The visualization I urge here and in the next chapter follows the example of Jesus, who used parables to convey important concepts in vivid ways. For example, the story of the Good Samaritan in-spires us beyond the lethargic sense of duty we feel in response to the verbal mandate to "love your neighbor as yourself." Jesus never directed his hearers to seek inner communication with the Good Samaritan as a spirit guide. Nor did he avoid using imaginary characters in memorable stories merely because demon worshipers in false religions also rely upon mental imagery. Similarly, I do not refuse to make *godly* use of this powerful technique just because someone else's ungodly abuse of it has perverted the technique.

# 6

# Use the Heart's Eye

When God's Son entered the stream of human history, we read that the Word (Jesus Christ) became flesh and lived among us and we beheld his glory (John 1:15). So also word pictures live and impact us more vividly than do mere word abstractions. We turn now to their use as a powerful tool for solving a wide variety of problems that people may bring to you as a counselor or a friend.

THE CONCEPT. The apostle Paul took for granted that mental seeing is therapeutic believing. He wrote to his beloved Ephesian Christians: "I pray also that the eyes of your heart may be enlightened in order that you may know the hope to which he has called you . . ." (Eph. 1:18). The Greek word for "heart" also translates as "mind or understanding." Paul here advocates godly use of our mind's eye to deepen our inward knowing of God's truth and thus find encouragement.

Long centuries before Paul, another man of God wrestled to make sense of the extreme anguish in his life. God seemed far off to Job as long as he merely recited his head knowledge about him. But he marked the dawning of insight at the end of his ordeal in these words to God: "I had heard of You [only] by the hearing of the ear; but now my [spiritual] eye sees You" (Job 42:5, AMPLIFIED). Therapeutic visualization calls for creating in our imaginations experiences that imprint themselves within our memories and emotions as surely as anything that happens to us in the real world.

To *realize* means "to make real in our experience." The word implies that we cause our thinking to conform with what *is*. Places we hear about become "real" to us when we go there. We even say of emotional ordeals, "I've been there. We must *experience* concepts in order for them to move from head knowledge to heart knowledge within us. Ideas affect us only when we go beyond knowing *about* them into that more intimate kind of knowing that is used to

107

describe sexual intercourse between husband and wife. A husband certainly knows his wife, in the sense of being acquainted with her, before their wedding. But he discovers her in a deeper way—truly "knows" her—when they symbolize their one-flesh union sexually after their wedding. When we see something "in our mind's eye," we make it real to our sensory experience. We put ourselves into a living encounter with it.

I am not sure which is more accurate to say when we visualize a truth of God: that we *create* a picture of it, or that we let into our minds and hearts a reality that already exists and that God is eager to saturate into us.

## An Illustration

In 2 Corinthians 10:4–5, Paul teaches: "The weapons we fight with are not weapons of the world. . . . we take captive every thought to make it obedient to Christ."

Invisible weapons! Powerful results in our thought life! How might you as counselor take that bold promise of therapeutic results and make it work for a defeated Christian who seeks your help?

I am about to create a sort of mental movie that symbolizes the abstract and invisible weapons of spiritual warfare by weapons and tools that are concrete and visible and that we *have* seen. I will design a brief script reminiscent of John Bunyan's allegory, *The Pilgrim's Progress*. In the scenario I will depict these godly weapons irresistibly prevailing over some common enemies of God's purpose for our lives. The story literally shows me taking thoughts captive and bringing them to obedience under the Lordship of Christ:

> I picture three categories of unruly thoughts in my mind, opposing my knowledge of God's goodness. One is Irritability, which I see as a snarling, yapping dog. Another is Lust, a howling, clawing wildcat. Over one I throw a net labeled "self-control." The other I lasso around the neck with a rope called "contentment." With legs powered by bulging Holy Spirit muscles, I march toward the throne of Christ, dragging these two renegade captives. I leave them there under his control, where they become docile.
>
> From Christ I get a giant lift truck such as warehouse workers use to haul barrels. I see stenciled across its side "thankfulness." I

drive it back to my third enemy, a surly brown bear, named Discouragement, who sits heavily on my heart and refuses to budge. I clamp him with steel jaws and lift him away, thrashing and kicking ineffectively, and dump him also at the feet of Jesus, where Discouragement thrashes no more, but merely gazes, enthralled, into his Maker's eyes.

### Test Yourself

How did you respond to that mental cartoon? Did it arouse any positive emotion in you? Inspiration? Relief? Amusement? Or did it offend or bore you?

I find that roughly 20 percent of the people I counsel do not like imagery. Another 20 percent do not find it useful, even if not objectionable. But over half of my clients benefit significantly and swiftly from vivid visual descriptions of pertinent experiences. Mental movies allow us the same liberty we find in dreams and cartoons: to depict truths in ways that we cannot do physically. We can picture ourselves flying with an eagle's wings, as the Bible says, though we will never actually grow feathers.

I distinguish between visualizing and fantasizing. The word *fantasy* implies farfetched, bizarre, and grotesque misapplications of our God-given creative ability. Sexual fantasies, for example, typically dwell on violations of God's laws. People indulge in them for self-gratifying entertainment. The mental imagery I advocate calls for effort that results in a God-honoring improvement of ourselves.

Here is another illustration:

> After using the dramatic images of gold and honey to characterize the ordinances of the Lord, David ends one of his psalms with a guideline for our use of mental imagery: "May the words of my mouth and the meditation of my heart be pleasing in your sight, O Lord, my Rock and my Redeemer" (Ps. 19:14). One might think of "the words of my mouth" as the audio component of a videotape. "The meditation of my heart" could add the visual dimensions of shape and color and movement.

Do you consider yourself a visually oriented person? Do you find that for you "seeing is believing"? If so, read on in this chapter to get some ideas that can stir your own creative juices as you assist other persons.

On the other hand, does the whole subject leave you disinterested? Then you might want to move on now to the exciting techniques of "logical analysis" presented in chapter 7.

### Objections to Visualization

Have you heard it said that Christians should have nothing to do with visualization? Let's take a look at these objections. Some people have written against visualization recently, on the basis that Eastern religions and occult practices make considerable use of it. These criticisms are well summarized in the book *The Seduction of Christianity* (Hunt and McMahon 1985). Their objections are well answered in a subsequent book, *Seduction?? A Biblical Response* (Reid et al. 1986).

In this book I have sought to show godly uses of visualization techniques and the scriptural precedents for doing so. It seems to me that critics who rule out the exercise of imagination just because false religions use a similar process may as well rule out prayer for the same reason. And will they excise Psalm 1 from the Bible because it urges us to meditate day and night, as do some idolatrous faiths? Visualization, like prayer and meditation, can be filled with wrong content and applied to evil purposes. But bad use by some does not make them bad tools any more than the possibility of committing murder with a knife leaves us only spoons with which to lawfully butter our bread. We are to apply these powerful tools to the holy process of glorifying God and engrafting his truth into our minds and hearts.

## The Technique

Educators tell us that we retain maybe 30 percent of what we hear, 60 percent of what we both hear and see, and 90 percent of what we hear and see *and* immediately use. Well-designed learning experiences therefore employ audiovisual materials as well as exercises for students to do right away, like filling blanks in questions about some segment of the material just presented.

You can actively involve people mentally and emotionally with a concept when you help them imagine something happening with it and them that includes their five senses. Suppose, for example, that a young woman in Christian work feels burned out; God is not real to her anymore and Christianity has lost its excitement. She needs a quick refresher. You might take her back to her first love for Christ with guided imagery like this:

> Tell her to see herself walking barefoot on a sandy beach of the Sea of Galilee. The air is fresh and fragrant. A cool breeze rustles her hair and clothing. The moist, smooth sand feels good under her feet as she digs her toes into it.
>
> As she walks along contentedly, she gradually notices that she is following another set of footprints in the sand, larger than her own. She pauses to look up, and there, about a hundred yards ahead of her, she sees an attractive man beckoning her and calling out magnetically, "Follow me!" He then turns and continues his walk. With a surge of excitement she realizes, "It's Jesus!" She looks back down at his tracks and resumes her walk, lengthening her stride so she fits each of her steps into one of his. She thrills to the thought, "I am following Jesus! And I have never felt so *alive* before!"

That's pretty much how you do it—you describe scenes and actions and sensory inputs that convey truths as would an artist rather than a scientist. To put it in technical terms, you add analogical representation to digital descriptions of factual information. That's what you do when you refer to a heavy object as "a backbreaker," along with reporting that "it weighs 72.4 kilograms."

I use mental imagery that causes to happen in people's felt experience and mental vision something universally true of the Bible's description of man's relationship with God. I make sure it also fits the need currently aroused in the person I am talking to. I especially reach for the hidden, root need behind the pain that the client presents on the surface. For example, one woman said she needed to learn how to be more loving. Because she cried as she said that, I recognized that her deeper need was to experience being held and comforted on the lap of a father like God—patient, unhurried, and understanding. (Incidentally, I do not try to *be* that comforter, either physically or emotionally. I avoid hugging, caressing or saying "I love you" to the people I counsel. It complicates things and risks the objectivity of my professional relationship to them.)

When I used guided imagery to describe this woman sitting on God's lap, with her tears soaking into the garments on his chest, she really let loose with tears as she experienced a deep conviction of God's receiving, comforting, and being a father to her.

The key is to select pictures and actions in which clients can see themselves not only actively obeying scriptural assignments, but also at other times passively receiving what God does *to* them. Both aspects are as important to Christian obedience as inhaling and exhaling are to breathing.

### Anticipate

The word *anticipate* means literally "to take before." By seeing something true to the character of Christ as if it were currently happening, we take hold of it and make it our inheritance before it happens.

Romans 8:16–17 speaks of us as God's children and "heirs of God and co-heirs with Christ." And Paul in Philippians joins that concept with another vivid visual metaphor he uses elsewhere, that of himself as a runner in a race: "I press on to take hold of that for which Christ Jesus took hold of me" (Phil. 3:12b).

We are not to wait for God to display all his glory in front of us before we say, "Wow!" Rather, we are to glorify him *now*. That means seeing the best we can in our imaginations what we can hardly wait to experience in reality.

### Stubborn Problems

Some of the most powerful therapy uses visualization to resolve some extremely difficult and painful human emotional problems. Particularly with memories of childhood abuse, visualization comes in handy to relive those memories in ways that can replace their original confusion and bitterness with loving memories consistent with God's original purposes.

Several authors have written helpful books on this powerful therapeutic procedure. For example, David Seamands's *Healing of Memories* (1985) is a particularly useful presentation consistent with vitality therapy (as are all of that author's works with mine).

When you design imagery that includes Jesus in a painful past event, describe him as absorbing the hurts, comforting the sufferer, ministering to the offender in response to the forgiving request of the victim, and finally promoting reconciliation between the alienated parties.

Christ died to take our sins away and came to turn back the hearts of children to their earthly fathers (Mal. 4:6). He urged in his model prayer that we forgive our debtors—just as he has forgiven us. We cannot even begin to pray the Lord's Prayer unless we acknowledge our solidarity as brother and sister with those tormentors who have wronged us. Being equally created in God's image, we can approach God only by calling him "our" Father.

## A Counselor's Deepening of Faith

Leading someone else through a prayerful drama of the healing power of Christ also does much to deepen the *counselor's* understanding and worshipful appreciation for the biblical message. Here are some further examples of how I have used this technique in my own life:

### Christ Died for My Sins

For years I knew in my head that Christ died for my sins and that I needed a Savior. However, though I had accepted Christ as my Savior and become a born-again Christian, I could not honestly say, along with people whose testimonies I heard, that I appreciated Christ for having taken a heavy load of sin off my shoulders. I had basically added Jesus to my life and thought of him as a companion. Yes, I delighted in worshipping him as my Lord, but what I lacked was a felt sense of the awfulness of my sins. I decided to use visualization to make real to my heart's experience that which I already had consented to in my statements of faith.

Fragments of Scripture and hymns helped me. I especially remembered a phrase from the hymn *Man of Sorrows, What a Name:* "Guilty, vile and helpless we; spotless Lamb of God was He." So I visualized myself standing in front of Jesus, his hands out toward me and inviting me to give him my sin. I pictured my corrupt nature as black poison dissolved throughout my bloodstream, contaminating my entire inner being. Yet Jesus stood there, saying, "Give me your sin."

I stretched my hands toward his arms and saw all the black poison in me concentrated into my fingertips. My nails became hypodermic needles. As I jabbed them forward, penetrating into the veins of Christ's forearms, he drew my poison into his bloodstream. It *all* went in. He took it from me and absorbed it into himself. He doubled over, screaming out in agony, and then crumpled to the ground, dead. His body sank slowly into the ground as into quicksand.

I was left alone except for an auditorium of heavenly beings standing around, silently stunned, knowing that I had killed the spotless Lamb of God. I felt guilty, vile, and helpless. I was in trouble and utterly alone—absolutely at the mercy of this incensed throng who knew and loved the One I had murdered! Worse than the angels, who probably wanted to tear me apart, I wondered with terror, "What will the Father think?"

After an ominous few minutes of silence, the earth began to rumble and stir in the place where Jesus had fallen. Suddenly the crust broke and Jesus exploded from the ground with a shout and a dazzling shower of light and praise and Hallelujahs! The crowd around me roared with ecstasy at his resurrection glory. He was victorious over death! He was pure and clean. My ugly blackness had stayed under the ground where death filtered it out. Jesus had carried it into the grave for me and left it there. Then he came back out without it—and now stood facing me.

The risen Jesus grinned at me, then seized me by the shoulders, saying, "Come here, dead clay." He breathed powerfully into my lungs, filling them as he had done at the original creation of Adam from dust. I remembered also how he had breathed on his disciples, telling them to receive the Holy Spirit. In place of that load of poison he had sucked out of my body, the Savior gave me the breath of life out of his own resurrection vitality! It surged within me! As I imagined this, I tingled with energy. I saw myself inhale deeply of my Lord's mighty breath and shout at the top of my lungs, "Hallelujah! What a Savior!"

Jesus then stepped back from me and said he had to get the rest of me clean. He turned a hose on me and washed me with his own cleansing blood, which abounded in unlimited supply. He showered and drenched me with it. I saw it as clear, not red, and strong with solvent power. He reached over and ruffled my hair, then laughingly scrubbed and doused and soaked me from head to toe, until he exclaimed triumphantly, "There, that ought to do it!" All of this he did to peals of laughing approval from the cloud of witnesses.

Then Jesus took away my old, soggy, threadbare clothing and put on me some lovely, white, new robes of righteousness. He told me that I had now been made holy.

Throughout this imagery I sobbed and I laughed. I was experiencing a transaction with Jesus as *Savior*. This engrafted into my soul the reality of what he had done. I finally permeated the membrane of doubt separating my head and heart. Now all of me—

mind, will, and emotions—consents together with my spirit: "I *know* Jesus as Savior and Lord!"

### Hephzibah

In the fall of 1983, I went on a seventeen-day "stress camping" experience in the North Woods wilderness. The second day into it I wanted to quit. My muscles ached from endless monotonous hours of backpacking. The straps dug into my shoulders. My thighs felt bruised from the relentless lifting of step after step all day long. I awoke the morning of the third day thinking that I would tell the group leader that I had to drop out. I planned to say that I had good intentions but not the stamina of a young person—and I was foolish to have bitten off more than I could chew.

However, I had deliberately come so as to practice persevering through precisely this kind of discouragement. I had benefitted greatly from a similar trip in the spring of 1976, so I knew it was tough but worthwhile. I urgently wanted an unforgettable meeting with the Living God in that wilderness crucible. So I made one last try, just before dawn that third day, as I awoke and began to pray by writing in my journal.

I often pray with more sense of reality by writing, using a variation of imagination techniques. I first write out a sentence or two to God, then fill in an answer from God—what he seems to be saying as I follow the command to "be still" and know that he is God (Ps. 46:10). What I "hear" from God generally surprises me. Too often my praying consists of my firing machine-gun requests at God without pausing to listen. This is what happened that fall day in 1983:

> That painful morning I wrote, "God, please give me something to go on today. If I can just see something of beauty, something to delight in, I think I can make it." Then, in one of those rare two or three times in my life when I would say that God spoke to me, I felt a gentle, playful presence near me and the answer coming as I wrote it down: "My son, let *me* delight in *you* today."
>
> I looked at the words in awe. How simple and yet profound. Of course! The God of all creation had created me for his pleasure. Since he is a Father and I his child, he delights in every little toddling movement I make. Even when my behavior is ungraceful and ungrateful, he marvels at his handiwork in me. I felt a surge of adrenaline with the thought that everything I did that day could bring

pleasure to the God of the universe. Talk about meaning and purpose! I could hardly wait for the day. And I had no further impulse to quit during that entire arduous trip.

In Isaiah 62:2, 4 we read: "... you will be called by a new name. ... No longer will they call you Deserted. ... But you will be called Hephzibah ... for the LORD will take delight in you. ..." My Bible's footnote tells me that *Hephzibah* means "my delight is in her," speaking of Israel. Just as it is more blessed to give than to receive, it afforded me more meaning, confidence, and purpose in life to *bring* delight to God than to have him entertain or serve me or give delight to me.

### Will a Man Rob God?

I next decided to apply the powerful techniques of visual praying to the matter of my mental and emotional purity. I realized how— just as drug addicts get high on the chemicals they abuse—I created highs for myself by mood-altering experiences. I did this by thinking vengeful or lustful thoughts. I did it, too, by loving to hear stories of people in authority who acted unjustly, so that I could justify my thrill of anger at them. Though I had prayed for years that God would take these unholy addictions from me, I still had them in a strength that noticeably weakened my spiritual vitality.

I went back to the concept that I had earlier experienced: that God had created me for his pleasure. I pondered over what in particular about me could bring delight to him. It dawned on me that God had already given me a giant clue, in what Jesus referred to as the first and greatest commandment: "Love the Lord your God with all your heart, and with all your soul, and with all your mind" (Matt. 22:37). That told me that God wanted especially for his pleasure *my* capacity to feel pleasure. That concept tied in with another for me: "Do not offer the parts of your body to sin, as instruments of wickedness, but ... to him [God] as instruments of righteousness" (Rom. 6:13).

I recognized that the crucial part of my body involved in those aroused emotional states was some intricate interplay of brain tissue, secretions, nerve impulses, heartbeat—a whole complex that I could lump together under the informal designation "emotional arousal mechanism." I realized that this capacity was particularly important to God, since he wanted my emotional arousals to connect me more closely to him. He wanted my delight to be in him, just as his delight was in me. That is Father-child intimacy—what any father's heart yearns for with his child. And I suddenly realized I had stolen that from God every time I had picked one of those ungodly subjects of anger, lust, worry, fear, or greed with which to inflame myself. Those were idolatries, disloyalties to the God who eagerly awaited my delight in him. I could now see clearly why God in the Old Testament frequently referred to Israel's departures from him as "adultery."

I visualized God as a playful, creative workman, having designed me with this intricate mechanism for emotional arousal. I saw him waiting eagerly for his workmanship—me—to respond in the way he designed it: for *his* pleasure. Instead I had dispersed my emotions into the air, toward objects that are not God. No wonder Satan is called "the ruler of the kingdom of the air" (Eph. 2:2)!

To discover how my selfish action affected God, I visualized looking at his face. He appeared crestfallen, like a child who has just had his fondest hopes dashed. He seemed sad, bereaved, grief-stricken. Always before, in my impure indulgences, I had imagined God angry at me for having them. When I saw him sad and disappointed, I burst into deep sobs. It broke my heart to think that I could wound God, to see that his feelings were as fragile as those of an innocent, unspoiled child. I felt horrified that I could cheat the eager, childlike Creator. I regretted diverting away from him the joy that he anticipated. For the first time in my life I felt sorrow over my wrongdoing, instead of rushing to apologize just because I felt in danger of being bawled out.

That powerful quarter-hour experience deprived my sinful habits of probably 50 percent of their power in my life. I still have further to go, but this therapeutic experience, created by using visualization, did more to renew my mind than the sum total of past promises I had made, and readings, tapes, and sermons I had ingested during decades of piety.

### Jesus as Organ Donor

The next imagery could help people who need assurance of salvation because of their difficulty in believing that God can really accept them. They consider themselves too bad, guilty, or dirty. Start off agreeing with the person rather than saying things like, "Oh, you're not too bad for God to accept." Such people have their focus all wrong. They look upon *their* character as the basis for

God's acceptance or rejection. But the Bible points to *God's* character as providing that basis. John 3:16 tells us that God "so loved the world," not that he found the world so irresistibly adorable.

Please avoid the error of a pastoral psychologist I know who tells people that the Bible says we are better than we think we are, and thus that it is only our low self-esteem that keeps us from knowing that we are doing the best we can. Scripture makes very plain that we can never be good enough to earn God's favor. We can only rely on the undeserved initiative that he takes on our behalf. This is the meaning of grace, a poorly understood concept that can be clarified by telling this vivid story:

> You know, you're right. Your very nature is absolutely incompatible with God's. You are like an arm torn from one body and now a candidate to be grafted onto God's body. But tissue typing shows it just won't work. His immune system would reject you. His nature is holy, pure, and unselfish; yours is rebellious, impure, and filled with self.
>
> But God wants you sewn onto him, so he has to supply a remedy that you cannot. What he needs to find is an organ donor who will provide connective tissue that can go between you and him. This tissue must be compatible both with God's nature and with human nature. You need a God-man to serve as organ donor, though it will cost him his life.
>
> But look, Jesus has already sacrified his life and made his connective tissue available! It is now up to you to accept his offer. Note what your refusal would mean. Even if you say such noble-sounding words as: "I am not worthy of it," the fact remains that he made the gift. If you turn it down, you are making light of his offer, unwilling to let him have the satisfaction he sought by laying down his life.

How fitting to that imagery are these hymn words:

> Just as I am, without one plea,
> But that Thy blood was shed for me,
> And that Thou bidd'st me come to Thee,
> O Lamb of God, I come, I come.

## A Photo Album

Here follow a variety of short mental pictures useful in different situations. (They resemble the quips and stories presented in chapter 3 on reframing.) I offer them as examples to stir your own creativity.

## Casting Our Cares

If a man prays to let go of lust, I might suggest that we borrow a concept from 1 Peter 5:7, and I quote it to him: "Cast all your anxiety on him [Jesus] because he cares for you." I tell him that the Greek word here translated "cast" represents the kind of vigorous action that Olympic shotputters use when they fling that sixteen-pound ball away from themselves with all their might. They even let out loud grunts of effort, which mark their intense determination to get it as far from themselves as they can.

I guide this man into seeing himself emphatically flinging gobs of black tarry lust away from himself to Jesus, who grabs them and puts them behind him into the lake of fire. Here they are incinerated and cannot "crawl back out" to harass the man.

Then I turn to pictures of the cleansing operation as laid down in 1 John 1:7: ". . . the blood of Jesus, his Son, purifies us from all sin." I symbolize this scrub-down with voluminous suds and water, like from a hose or shower or waterfall, with maybe a platoon of angels laughing and singing as they brush off every trace of tar.

Next are pictured some new garments of purity in place of the man's old, polluted garments of immorality. Ephesians 4:22–24 gives us the basis for this rich imagery. I ask the man to see himself standing unashamed in front of Jesus now, clothed in clean white robes of righteousness, representing the new attitudes of holiness engrafted into his mind.

Then I ask the man what he thinks God would probably fill him with in place of the tarry lust. (I follow this idea as one of my key  principles: always show God as giving us something far more valuable and abundant in place of anything we give up in obedience to him.) I suggest to the man that God gives the genuine article that lust counterfeits, namely the experience of joy in loving attachments to other persons. I might symbolize joy for him by amplifying the picture that Jesus used in John 4:14—a spring of living water bubbling up inside him and flowing over with a gurgling, happy, irrepressible vitality that benefits others.

## 7:58 and 41 Seconds

One morning I had to keep repeating to myself that reading from my watch several times during each lap I jogged around the track. I had started my mile run at that exact time and would need to subtract it from the reading at the end of my run in order to know how long the mile took me. I noticed that if I did not repeat "7:58 and 41" often enough between other thoughts, those newer ones tended to crowd out my "7:58 and 41."

How similar is that experience to our memories of past hurts! We keep them fresh by frequently repeating them. But when we create new and pleasant "memories" *as if* they had happened, repeating them frequently and vividly at the expense of our ancient bitter ones, the old ones tend to lose their mental stranglehold.

I asked a client in one of our counseling sessions how she would be different today if she had different memories. She answered that she would now be a confident, well-adjusted, outgoing person if her father had exerted manly leadership in her childhood home, instead of letting her hyper-critical mother dominate. I asked her to imagine that a new medical procedure became available—a painless, completely safe magnetic reorientation of molecules in a small portion of her brain. It would affect nothing else in her mental processes except those debilitating memories of childhood hurts and disappointments. The medical procedure would replace those with memories of Dad's exercising loving yet firm leadership in the home, while Mom relaxed in the security of his confident competence and therefore was continually blessing rather than berating the kids.

However, I made a mistake in that session that I have sought to avoid since: I asked this client if she would be willing to use such a procedure if it were available. She answered *no*, that it would have been nice to have things the way I described, but that, after all, reality is reality and Mom and Dad would never have acted that way. She was saying that she just had to accustom herself to living with her disappointment forever.

I now realize that I did not need this woman's verbal consent to put into her mind some new memories. People come to counseling to be influenced for the better, as the counselor sees fit. By asking this woman's permission, I simply invited her resistance. In bold Christian witnessing, we do not ask people if they want to hear the best news in the world. If they expect something "religious" that they don't want to hear, they may answer *no*. Then, if we go ahead, we're being rude. How much better to lead in with the very information we want to deliver. For example, we could say, "Have you ever heard the good news that God loves you and has a wonderful plan for your life?" There, within the question, we plant the new thought like a seed that we hope will take root and grow.

### Changing Memories

The new and appealing memory pictures that we plant in people's minds have a chance of growing there, especially if they intrigue the people enough to ruminate on them again and again. Then they come to compete with the old, bitter memories and eventually crowd them out. We can literally change our personalities by changing our memories. Not that our memories *determine* our personalities. Rather, they reflect them and serve to justify some inner vows by which we have been living. Therefore, when we change our memories, of necessity we have to let go of our tendency to continue justifying our way of living in enmity with others. Below are several examples:

1. *"Friend of Smokey the Bear."* A certain woman tended to react too sharply and readily to her husband's criticisms. She had in the past week (at my suggestion) stopped these overblown responses and instead experimented with giving soft answers to each of his attacks. She might say, "You're probably right," or "I'll have to think about that," or "Thank you for letting me know." The woman reported less volatility between her husband and herself when she did that. I had originally likened her soft answers to a gentle rain that decreases the hazard of forest fires in a dry woods, so I later complimented her for being "a friend of Smokey the Bear" (the advertising symbol for preventing forest fires).

2. *Fill in the blanks.* A male client complained of difficulty urinating in public restrooms. He said he had been that way ever since one time as a child when his father took him into a roadside restroom while on a long trip and got impatient when the boy who "had to go" then couldn't do so in the bathroom.

I asked the man to go back in his imagination to that childhood setting and picture something very funny happening in the midst of the scene, which he used to think of only as tense and awkward. He thought a moment, and then a grin spread over his face and he laughed. He said that he pictured himself urinating so vigorously that it was like a high-pressure fire hose squirting wildly all over that restroom—to the amazement of his father, who cried out, "All right, all right, enough already!"

The man reported to me two weeks later having had only about 25 percent of his previous difficulty. "I just remember that hilarious scene and it really relaxes me," he said.

Notice that I did not tell this man *how* to solve his problem but merely gave him a way to solve it himself. He filled in the blank when I suggested he add something funny to the mental picture that typified his problem. Humor, of course, is often a relaxing antidote to anxieties that impede normal physiological functions.

3. *"I am the vine, you are the branches."* A woman I was counseling recalled with bitterness some childhood tormentors who had made fun of her appearance. She wanted to forgive these former enemies, so I decided to use imagery that would fulfill the Scripture about doing good for enemies, such as by providing them with a refreshing cup of cold water.

I had the woman view herself as a section of a tree limb that was passing on sap from the trunk, representing Christ, out to the twigs and leaves, representing her former classmates, at the end of the limb. They had once made her not a part of them, but now in her mental picture they held a position absolutely dependent upon their vital connection with her. In faithfully passing on to them the sustenance they needed, she emotionally connected herself with them in a giving, loving way.

I had this client describe her classmates as thriving and blossoming *because* she did her part. This was completely opposite from her revenge fantasies, in which she would have loved to have her enemies dependent on her, so that she could *hurt* them. In this godly imagery, she imitated her heavenly Father, who causes his favors to fall on all his children, the deserving and the undeserving.

4. *New sound track.* Clients often object to using mental imagery to revise old memories. They say, "It's just a trick," because it does not really make the painful memories go away. I agree with them, but then I use the analogy of a recording artist I once heard, who sang the same song in different melodic variations several times over on one sound track. Each new track, added to the old ones, made the song different. He did not need to erase the old in order to add the new. In fact, I agree further with the objectors by saying that we cannot erase human memories. What we *can* do, by adding new memories on top of the old ones, is make a crown of beauty out of ashes (Isa. 61:3).

5. *Melted Velcro.* Velcro is the commercial name for a plastic fastening material composed of miniature hooks on one side that grab onto tiny loops on the other, fuzzy side. I once had an item with a defective Velcro closure. The fuzzy side had been heated

somehow so that all the loops melted together into one smooth, glassy surface. The hooks could not grab onto it but just slid off every time I tried to engage them.

I use that description with clients who readily become provoked into an argument by some person in their lives. I have them picture themselves as fuzzy pieces of Velcro that have melted under the radiant warmth of God's love so that they are smooth instead of "hookable." Then, when their provocateurs come at them with inciting statements or taunts, the "hooks" just slide right off.

I give people soft-answer sentences they can use to stay "smooth" instead of "fuzzy." In answer to criticisms, the smooth person can say, "That sounds like something I'd better correct," or "Thank you for letting me know." Even in answer to being called "a jerk," the melted person might merely ask, "Specifically what do I do that in your eyes makes me a jerk?"

6. *The prodigal's brother.* I like to use this one when I talk with people who have bitter memories of childhood clashes with a sibling. If they know the parable of the Prodigal Son (Luke 15:11–32), I have them imagine a variation of it, and with themselves in the role of older brother. This time, when the prodigal returns home, his brother welcomes him. He joins in the celebration, shouting to the whole household with delight, "Hey, gang! He's back! The family is complete again! Drop everything else you are doing! Dad, come and see who's here!" Then, with tears streaming down his cheeks, he joins in a triple hug with Dad and his little brother.

It helps people to relive the story this way, even if they were once the prodigal mistreated by a rigid, unloving older brother or sister. Or, if they were that older sibling who treated a younger one without compassion, this retelling helps clear the way for them to reconcile with the loved one. Retelling the story the way it should have been engrafts a mental picture of both the Father-son cooperation that Jesus demonstrated in his relationship with God and the spirit of brotherhood we enjoy as children in God's family.

7. *The ninety and nine.* Jesus sketched a word picture about a shepherd's joy at having his one lost sheep out of a hundred restored to the fold (Matt. 18:12–14). He used this metaphor to convey God's infinite love for each individual. I find I need to modernize the imagery to help clients who may have a hard time feeling accepted by God, yet have no experiences involving sheep to make the story relevant for them.

I first find out if they ever had a beloved pet—a dog or cat or perhaps a pig they raised for a 4-H contest—some animal to which they devoted themselves at some time in their lives. Then I ask them to imagine that the pet is lost and they go searching for it. They visualize looking all over the neighborhood for hours, until finally late in the day they hear its bark, meow, oink, or whatever. They rush to the pet and rescue it from a trapped, uncomfortable position. How happy both owner and pet are to be reunited!

I ask the clients how they would feel about getting that pet back. They usually describe tearful joy. Then I ask them if they think God is any less loving a Master.

8. *Dead to sin.* In Romans 6, Paul refers to Christians as having died to sin. He likens baptism to burial with Christ, then tells us to consider ourselves dead to sin but alive to God in Christ, through whom we, too, are raised to new life. I could use various imagery to describe the unresponsiveness of "the dead." For example, I remember being with my father twenty minutes after he died. I took his hand, still warm and pliable, and shook it. I said, "Dad! Dad! I have a joke for you!" My father always had a ready ear for jokes, so that line would invariably get his attention away from anything else. This time he did not respond—no flicker of an eye, no animation on the face—*dead.* I could not get him to budge. In the same way are we to be unflickering to lusts, compulsions, or temptations that used to get an automatic rise out of us.

9. *The image of God.* Discouraged people usually need a sense of purpose for their lives. When they grump, "I don't know why God even bothered to make me," I congratulate them on having raised a very good point. I then mention that we know God made each of us in his image and therefore that he intends to say something slightly different to the world through each individual. Next I ask, "What message do you most want the world to get from *you* about God?" I offer a few suggestions, such as:

"You matter to me."

"I made you and I know you."

"I'm glad you're here!"

"I enjoy you."

"I love you."

"I'm in this with you."

"I've been there."

"I will never leave you or forsake you."

10. *Decisions, decisions.* As a counselor I often quote that Jesus "for the joy set before him endured the cross . . ." (Heb. 12:2). I may also mention that the root Greek words behind our word *enthusiasm* literally mean "God in us." That leads to the point that God guides us into making decisions more by joy than by duty or obligation.

Suppose a girl has a hard time deciding between two boyfriends. I might borrow a concept from the story of King Solomon, who proposed cutting a baby in half so that the two women who claimed the baby could each have a share (1 Kings 3:16–27). The real mother offered to give up the child rather than let him die, and she was awarded her son. In like manner, I have the undecided girl imagine that she has witnessed a terrible car accident in which both of these fellows were dragged from the wreckage, bleeding. I ask her first how the picture makes her feel, then what it makes her feel like doing.

My questions focus her attention on the drama and emotion of the story. Then I ask her to continue the story—what does she see herself doing next? Only later do I ask which man she saw herself going to first in her mind's eye. I do not tell her that he is the one she really loves. She is still too ready to stay publically undecided, so as to delay giving up an option she would like. It is enough that I have helped her to know her own mind better, so that when she does make a decision, she has already been there at the choice point she faced in my accident story.

11. *"Honor your father and mother."* That is ". . . the first commandment with a promise—'that it may go well with you and that you may enjoy long life on the earth'" (Eph. 6:2–3). Much of the material that people bring to a counselor includes unfinished business from relationships with their parents. Often the parent failed to "earn" the child's honor. Nevertheless, the grown-up children of inadequate parents can still garner the blessing by honoring the parents for the *position* they held, regardless of the *personalities* they brought to it.

To guide people in mentally honoring their parents, I might have them imagine that they put on a surprise banquet at which their parents are the guests of honor. Or I have them imagine themselves saying some complimentary things at a parent's graveside.

Sometimes I ask, "When were you most proud of your mom or dad?" Even reciting a specific, minute incident tends to break the ice of bitterness and institute a new pattern of warm gratitude toward parents, which produces a benign blessing effect on a child of any age. I believe that "honoring" our parents creates a chemical reaction inside our bodies that counteracts the corrosive effect of any acidic bitterness, whether or not the bitterness is justified by the facts.

I actually told one such specific, positive memory to my father some years before he died—thereby taking pains to give him his eulogy while he could hear it. It went like this:

> Dad, I remember one time when I was about three years old, that you were home, sitting in your favorite chair, reading the newspaper. Mom was working in the kitchen, and I was pretending to run our vacuum cleaner over the living room rug. But its cord was coiled up and I just made motor sounds with my mouth.
>
> And, Dad, I remember that you laid your newspaper down into your lap, and with a voice of gentle strength smiled at me and said, "Den, why don't you uncoil the cord, plug it in, and *really* vacuum?"
>
> I want you to know how proud I felt that my dad thought I could do real, useful work.

As I told my father that story, a tear came to his eye and he said, "I don't remember that incident, but thank you so much for telling me." Months later, our whole, big family of three generations gathered for Thanksgiving. As we reminisced about old times, my father turned to me and asked, "Den, do you remember the time that you pretended to vacuum our living room rug, and I suggested you plug the cord in and *really* vacuum?" I could hardly choke back my own tears as I answered simply, "Yeah, Dad, I remember." The "memory" that he had not remembered became his because I planted it in his mind and it took root and grew there. Visualizing such positive memories can "honor your father and mother" long after they are gone.

12. *By grace, not works.* I sometimes describe faith as being like power steering. When driving a car, I put forth a small effort in the direction I want to turn, and the power-steering mechanism boosts that into a much greater effect than I exert. My faith is like that.

Though there is a very small amount of effort on my part, God's response of grace boosts and amplifies my little bit. This carries further the meaning of Jesus' call for mustard-seed faith. A tiny investment from us in the direction of obeying God gives him something to build on, which he apparently will not do from scratch, that is, without our little input.

"You see, at just the right time, when we were still powerless, Christ died for the ungodly" (Rom. 5:6). Our very helplessness is a precondition for grace. Sometimes obedience calls for passive acceptance on our part. We can receive the gift of God only by *letting* ourselves be loved (see Eph. 2:8–9).

## "I Saw the Light"

People often express sudden breakthroughs in their understanding in visual terms, even when they have not used visualization. "I saw the light. It dawned on me, I never *looked* at it that way before," they exclaim. Sometimes direct challenges to inconsistencies in their logic have the power to promote these flashes of insight, as we will see in the next chapter.

# 7

# Challenge Logic

*Devoted mother.* A mother brought her ten-year-old son for counseling. She said that he had eagerly gone to camp the summer before, but had called home after two days, saying he could not stand to be away. He pleaded so pathetically that Mom drove to camp and brought him home, even though she believed the camp experience would help him develop some healthy self-confidence. Now the boy wanted to go to camp again and Mom, fearing a repeat of the previous year, wondered what to do.

I asked this mother what she thought would happen if her son called from camp again, homesick, but this time she refused to pick him up and simply gave him her vote of confidence: "I'm sure you can handle it one way or another. I love you. Goodbye!" She said she would feel like a bad mother and could not bear the thought of leaving her son suffering on the other end of the phone, even if it would help him to learn how to work out his own problems.

I clarified that it really would create a terrible agony for *Mom* if she said *no* to her son's heartrending pleas. She agreed. Then I instructed her to turn to her son, look him in the eyes, and say, "I do not love you enough to suffer for you."

She flinched, tears filled her eyes, and a smile crossed her face as she said emphatically to her son, "I *do* love you enough to suffer for you. So I'm *not* coming up to get you early from that camp. If you don't like it there, that's your business. I'm letting *you* handle it."

This basically healthy family did not need a second appointment. No one engaged the boy in months of therapy for separation anxiety or oedipal issues. He did not become stigmatized or initiated into the role of disturbed child or mental patient. One incisive challenge to Mom's logic helped her to see for herself that she could sometimes exercise her devotion to her son's well-being better by firmness than by softness.

*Ambitious father.* A furious father brought his teenage son to see me because he was getting low grades in high school. The dad said that the horrible thing about his son's low grades was that the boy would never get into college and thus would never qualify for a really good job. I asked, "And the horrible thing about that?" The father sputtered as if I had just displayed raw imbecility by asking a question with such a self-evident answer. Nevertheless, he had to think a moment before he came up with, "Well, then he'll have a hard life."

I directed this father to make the following statements to his son: (1) "I am not willing to let you choose a hard life" and (2) "I can force you to have the kind of life I want you to have."

Next, before they could get into an argument over those lines, I had the son say back to his father, "I am going to prove that you cannot make me do anything, and I don't care what it costs me."

These exaggerated statements of their secretly held beliefs made each one a bit more open to my counseling. As their original positions came to feel less defensible to them, each hungered for some new, more acceptable viewpoint with which to fill the void. I asked the father if he really believed he could keep his son from having a hard life. When he agreed that he could not, I asked him what attitude he *could* take if his son foolishly created a hard life for himself. Dad finally grasped the meaning of healthy detachment when he said, "I can be there for him and let him know I care, but not interfere as if I *have* to have him turn out a certain way."

With the son I pursued the question of how much personal price he really would be willing to pay just to carry out his dedicated mission of proving that his dad could not boss him. Would he sacrifice financial prosperity simply because his father wanted him to succeed financially? When he laughed at that notion, I offered him the following statement as a kind of down payment on a future of healthy, friendly detachment from Dad: "I have decided to live a happy, successful life, even though my father wants me to."

*If only I were. . . .* A college student, given to perfectionism, worry, and depression, came to me in anxiety over the possibility that her latest boyfriend might jilt her, as the previous one had done. I asked her what in particular would make such a jilting a horrible experience for her. She said it would prove she was not attractive enough to keep a guy. Then I had her say, "If I were attractive enough, any guys I liked would *have no choice* but to continue going with me."

That challenge tickled her funny bone and set her to rethinking her outlook. It expressed the grandiosity that underlies people's woeful lament that they would be okay if only they were something that they don't think they are. Then others would be duty-bound to grant the esteem that these greedy perfectionists seek. This young woman had relied for security on the belief that "good enough" qualities or performances on her part would give her sovereign powers to override others' free will and compel them to do her bidding.

*Letting God down.* A friend came to me discouraged, feeling distanced from God because he had indulged in sexual fantasies over the weekend. He said he felt as if he had let God down. I invited him to say aloud, "Before that, I was propping God up. Poor, feeble God needs me as his secure foundation."

Similarly, a family member once told me that God seemed far away from her. She asked, "How do I get God to come near again?" I told her to say aloud, "It's up to me to bring God out of hiding."

THE CONCEPT. Each of the above situations has in common a similar kind of punch line, consisting of one or more jarring statements of an unexamined belief or policy by which the client has been living. These pithy statements challenge the logic of the person who brings a complaint to the counselor. They put into clear, direct sentences the vaguely formulated viewpoints that people live by without realizing it. The best challenges take the form of short mottoes or slogans such as could appear on a T-shirt or bumper sticker. Exaggeration often helps underscore the challenge, sometimes in a progression of increasingly outlandish statements of the faulty logic.

I once found a tuft of grass growing out of a small crack in a huge granite boulder on the shore of Lake Superior. The rock was destined to split as more living plants found their way into the crack and relentlessly pressed their roots against its sides. In the same way, logical challenges wedge their way into discrepancies in people's thinking, widening the gap between two conflicting beliefs until the people cannot bear the inconsistency and therefore resolve it, usually in favor of the "sensible" alternative. Psychologists refer to this powerfully motivating mental discomfort as "cognitive dissonance." A counselor can arouse it to help people discover for themselves more workable ways of viewing their dilemmas.

## The Basic Technique

Here's a synopsis of how I apply the technique. First, I tell clients that I have a sentence I want them to repeat after me, to see if it sounds to them like an accurate statement of what they think and feel. Next, I say it. Then they repeat it, either verbatim or in words of their own that convey the same meaning. After pausing a second or two until I see their mental wheels stop turning, I ask, "True or false?" They answer one or the other, or else they debate it aloud by giving arguments for both sides until they come up with a conclusion.

You can tell when you have hit a bull's-eye with one of your logical challenges. People often get a look on their faces that reminds you of the combined relief, chagrin, and amusement someone shows upon hearing the solution to a puzzling riddle. It's the "Aha!" experience. They generally smile a recognition reflex. Their jaws may drop open. They may say, "Oh!" They sometimes cry. They frequently confirm the impact of the challenge with words like, "I never looked at it that way before." If they ever volunteer feedback to you some time after you have helped them, they typically say, "You have a way of wording things that goes right to the core of my problem."

This chapter will tell you how to hear the underlying beliefs implied in what people say and how they say it. It explains how to formulate these covert beliefs into punchy challenges, how to present them for maximum effect, and how to build on the results. Specific examples peppered throughout illustrate the procedure.

## How to Detect Faulty Beliefs

Some ways that people express their complaints offer better handles for logical challenges than do others. They drip with inconsistency and contradict other, more sound beliefs that you know the people also hold. Take, for example, a depressed Christian woman who says that God could not possibly love her. You know that she also believes that God so loved the world that he gave his only begotten Son. Your logical challenge will exploit the discrepancy between those two beliefs so that she decides for herself that God *does* love her.

People like this woman have generally not benefitted from the well-meant advice of family and friends who have insisted to her that God certainly loves her—she's not as bad as she thinks, she shouldn't be so hard on herself, and so on. Typically, the best absurdities to challenge have a strong tendency to draw you into giving some such predictable response. But you resist that impulse and recognize that this woman's "God cannot love me" implies "I have overwhelmed him"! She views her awfulness as so monumental that it has defeated the God of the universe. As previously mentioned, this kind of grandiosity underlies many of the complaints you can turn into logical challenges. Behind grandiosity you always find the ultimate unexamined belief innate in rebellious, proud human nature: "I will make myself like the Most High."

### Using the Clues

Challenging logic takes counselors thoroughly into the truth that Jeremiah expressed: "The heart is deceitful above all things, and it is exceedingly perverse *and* corrupt and severely, mortally sick! Who can know it?" (Jer. 17:9, AMPLIFIED). Well, with the discerning tool of logical challenges we can know some of it and can then expose it to the light and revise it to the right. The following

baker's dozen statements reflect some common hidden beliefs—
and thus the logical challenges that a counselor can present as he
or she begins to "know the heart" of someone who has come for help.

1. *"I can't bear to see someone else suffer."* This was the frame of
reference of the homesick camper's mother in the opening illustration of this chapter. Some counselors predictably and unhelpfully
respond to this on-the-surface compassionate anguish with such
attempts at comfort as: "Here, I'll spare you," or "You poor dear," or
"Don't worry. You are not causing as much pain as you think you
are." But the mother's statement reveals a deeper perspective: "My
own comfort is my first priority."

2. *"If only I. . . ."* You could fill in the blanks with such longings as
these: ". . . had been there; . . . had tried harder; . . . had done the
right thing; . . . were taller/shorter/younger/older/prettier." People
who lament in this way generally do not verbalize the specific magical
outcome they anticipate, but their conditional statement carries the
sweeping flavor of ". . . everything would be okay." Mistaken consola-
tions would take the form of: "Oh, you're fine the way you are." Or,
"You still could not have kept the tragedy from happening." Or, "You
did the best you could." Sufferers rarely take comfort from such words
unless they discover their meaning for themselves.

You might quickly help a client to do so by phrasing a logical
challenge of this variety: "Things would *have to* be the way I wish
they would be." With the college girl who was afraid of being jilted,
the challenge emphasized that guys would *have no choice* but to
admire her if only she were attractive enough. Thinking back to
George (the college sophomore whose father had died while George
was away on a trip), he might benefit from a well-timed challenge
like, "If only I had been there, Dad could not possibly have died."

3. *"I need to know I'm loved."* This implies, "You are obligated to
prove to me that I am loved—and you have not done it well enough
yet." You point out a generic connection here: "I need . . ." implies
"Others *must* provide. . . ."

4. *"People will think badly of me."* This means, "They have
nothing better to do than to think about me." The statement reveals a grandiosity behind the shyness. When people act timid,
they often flatter themselves that their awkwardness is a big deal
to other people.

5. *"Things always go against me"* translates as "I'm special."
After all, ordinary people fairly often have things work out the way

they prefer. So someone for whom this *never* happens must be extraordinary—singled out by society or fate or God for unusual treatment, therefore something of a celebrity.

6. *"Why did this have to happen to me?"* This question implies that God goofed. It holds in common with the preceding example the notion of privileged status, which ought to exempt the sufferer from the normal "slings and arrows of outrageous fortune" that mere mortals have to endure.

Here the counselor needs to walk a thin line between challenge and sarcasm. If you do not sense that the persons you counsel can stand a little tickling from you, do not play up the part about their considering themselves privileged characters. But do press them on the question of whether or not they think it could be that God, who usually knows what he's doing, perhaps committed a bit of a blunder in the situation under discussion. You hope, of course, to arouse people to such a statement of faith as: "No, he *always* knows what he's doing, and I'm sure he has a purpose in allowing this."

7. *"I should . . ."* implies "I can. . . ." Regrets by perfectionists often sound something like this: "I should have known the stock market was going to go down. Now I've blown it and lost hundreds of dollars. It's all my fault." Most comforters will say things like, "Don't be so hard on yourself. You couldn't have known. Even the world's best experts can't predict the stock market." But these comments miss the grandiosity that the perfectionistic self-punisher needs to face. Instead, you can ask that sufferer to pronounce a logical challenge: "It was fully possible for me to know ahead of time when the stock market was going to go down."

8. *"I don't want to hurt anybody's feelings."* This excuse for inaction, when confrontive action is called for, translates into a hidden belief (hence, a logical challenge): "They're too fragile to handle what I say." Timid restraint of proper bold action actually implies an insult to the person therefore not confronted.

9. *"I can't stand. . . ."* This statement implies "I deserve exemption." It fits with the common protest, "Why should this difficulty happen to *me?*" (see #6) and its cogent answer, "Why *not* you?" That exposes the prideful heart of the issue—the belief that one is entitled to special protection from hardships.

10. *"I don't want to live if I can't have X."* Perhaps X represents some loved person—a child, spouse, or fiancé whose loss is threatened, for whatever reason. On the surface this plaintive declaration

sounds like the height of devotion. But notice how it also contains an insult rooted in the announcer's feelings of superiority: "The rest of you jerks do not make my life worth living, and I certainly don't intend to devote my energies to improving *your* lot in life." This challenge contrasts the sufferer's pseudo-devotion to the self-less definitions of love that resound from Scriptures like 1 John and 1 Corinthians 13.

11. *"But what if my idea doesn't work?"* Fear of failure implies a prediction of savage treatment from others. When we shrink from trying our best because we predict failure, we secretly believe that people who discover our failure will ridicule, reject, or otherwise brutalize us. We do not rely on or even expect their goodwill. We also discount the fact that we have recovered from other failings in the past. One logical challenge for fear of failure might be this: "I am surviving now merely because I have not yet failed at anything I have ever undertaken." Others you could use are: "Even if I have rebounded from failures in the past, I surely cannot in the future," or, "My failures are a really big deal."

12. *"Why should I be the one to do all the changing?"* You often encounter this objection from one party to a conflict, especially if you are coaching that person to take some creative initiatives to resolve the conflict. Pose a challenge like this: "I don't want to make things better if the other party doesn't want to even more." Or, "Making things better is more of a chore than an honor." Or, "It doesn't matter much to me that I have it within my power to make things better."

13. *"I don't want to impose on anyone's kindness."* This apparent humility reveals an underlying anti-social independent spirit. It means, "I refuse to allow anyone else the satisfaction of doing something kind for me." Use this with people who won't accept favors, including your time and attention.

### Building a Chain of Challenges

Sometimes I like to design a Socratic sequence of logical challenges to unsettle people from a troublesome belief system. The handle I pick up on for my first challenge often represents an expression of disappointment by the client. Emotions of disappointment trace back to clients' unmet expectations, and those to their imposition of demands for what they want, and those to grandiose beliefs about who they are, and those to the root of all disruption:

rebellion against God. So I follow this sequence in developing an inductive chain of challenges: disappointment or fear—expectations—demands—grandiosity—displacing God. The following paragraphs give several common examples of this technique.

*Adult children of deficient parents.* In recent years an excellent movement has arisen to help grown-ups who, though they no longer have to cope with an alcoholic loved one, did have to do so years before in childhood and never quite got over the damaging effects of such tribulation. They often had to take on adult responsibilities in their households while still quite young, say eight to fifteen years. A similar situation was faced by youngsters who lost a parent to death, divorce, desertion, disease, or disability.

The conscientious children decided they would and *could* fill in the gap at least as well as the missing parent. To achieve this heroic ambition, they nurtured a mentality of stretching beyond their limited capabilities; in fact, they rarely acknowledged any such limits. These young people developed a sense of identity and security as volunteers for responsibilities not their own. Particularly if they hated parental conflict, these kids took it upon themselves to heal all interpersonal clashes and restore household harmony. Challenges to habitual thought patterns thus evolved must highlight the grandiose belief that these adult children, by diligent enough effort, can *compel* events to go the way they want them to.

In reflecting on their family-of-origin disharmony, these clients often verbalize their over-responsible orientation with such words as, "I feel like it's all *my* fault." This implies a traceable train of thought, which a counselor can suggest that the client say aloud as a thought-provoking progression of logical challenges. I like to help clients think through such challenges as those listed below by asking, after they repeat each one, "True or false?"

1. "It's my fault because I did not do everything I could to prevent the bad things that happened."
2. "If I had done the right thing, everything would be okay now."
3. "There *was* some right thing possible for me to discover and do that would surely have made everything better."
4. "If I had done the right thing, everything would *have* to be better now."
5. "Power is available to me to *make* everything be the way I want it to be."

6. "I am just like God."

*The obligation of romantic love.* Our society's glorification of romantic love seems to damage women in particular. They take on happily-ever-after expectations that leave them disappointed at the un-princelike forgetfulness of their real-life husbands. Underlying the complaints they express is the demand that their husbands recognize and meet their wishes without the wives having to ask.

As counselor, you can begin with that demand for mind-reading and progress logically to the ultimate destination—the godlike pretentions embedded in self-centered concepts of romantic love. Here are some logical challenges you can start with:

"If my husband really loved me, he would know what I want without my having to tell him."

"Love equips people with ESP." (If the woman does not recognize the term *ESP,* explain that it means "extra-sensory perception," the ability to read minds. Then restate the challenge, "Falling into true love equips lovers with a crystal ball.")

"*I* certainly know unfailingly everything *he* wants without his having to tell me."

"When I am loved, I have a *right* to the kind of treatment I want."

"I am entitled to loving treatment from my husband without effort on my part."

Next might follow a full sequence of *progressive* logical challenges you can use, based on the woman's quest for reassurance:

1. "If my husband really loved me, he would know what I want without my having to tell him."
2. "It is important for me to know that my husband loves me."
3. "If I tell him what I want and he does it, I have no way of knowing if he loves me or not."
4. "By *not* telling him, I can test to find out whether he loves me or not."
5. "I am in a position to test my husband and evaluate his performance as my lover."
6. "My position is one of authority over my husband."
7. "That puts me on a par with God."

*Fear of surrender to God.* A common complaint among Christians who seek help is their fear that, if they devote themselves 100 percent to God, he will cause or allow some horrible thing to happen in their lives. Well-meaning friends and relatives unwisely offer the standard knee-jerk reflex response, "No, he won't. Why, he's a loving Father who tenderly cares for his own." But I have found that fear lends itself well to the following, more penetrating sequence of logical challenges:

1. "Bad things can't happen to me as long as I don't surrender completely to God."
2. "My aloofness renders the God of the universe powerless over me."
3. "I am currently exercising considerable control over God's actions toward me. His sovereignty pales into insignificance when faced with my monumental stubbornness."
4. "My refusal is my salvation."
5. "God is more likely to hurt me if I surrender to him than if I don't."
6. "My surrender to God will trigger a latent bloodthirstiness on his part."
7. "God finds pleasure in torturing his creatures."
8. "My submission into the role of Christ's bride will reveal him to be a wife-abuser."
9. "Since I hold higher ethical standards than God does, I qualify to replace him."

*The unpardonable sin.* Clients who condemn themselves make prime subjects for logical challenges. These people have typically received Christ dozens of times, feeling clean and close to God for a while afterward, only to slump into despair upon thinking of themselves as too bad for God to forgive. If you have them say, in summary of their distress, "God *refuses* to forgive me," it will rattle them. It accurately reflects what they are saying, of course, but it does not emphasize what they want to emphasize. The challenge focuses on God, whereas their self-condemnation focuses on themselves. What sounds self-effacing is really self-centering.

The following string of challenges intensifies the switch from the clients' pathetic suffering to their stubborn refusal:

1. "I've been so bad that I have forfeited all rights to any merciful treatment from God."

2. "God has every right to wipe me out."
3. "Since he holds the power of life and death over me, he can do with me as he sees fit."
4. "He can, if he wishes, delay killing me and assign me some task as his servant."
5. "Since I am still living and breathing, I must already be on such an assignment from God."
6. "Since I still talk more about *my* badness than about *his* goodness, it shows that I have accepted neither God's forgiveness nor his assignment."
7. "Therefore, I do not acknowledge God's right to treat me in any way he decides."
8. "Since I can deny God his rights, I am above him."

Clients who complain that they can neither feel God's forgiveness, nor believe that God really loves them, nor rid themselves of guilt feelings for their sins, all thereby imply that they *could* live cleanly enough so that God would *have to* forgive them if they actually did. "I am too bad for God to accept me" implies that "if I were good enough, he would *have to* accept me." This notion grows out of a works-righteousness philosophy and a desire to "boast," as described in Ephesians 2:8–9. It reflects the strong-willed belief that people can, by their own exertion of will, acquire power to compel life, others, and even God to comply with their dictates.

*Snags in talking with you.* A middle-aged woman tells me she does not express herself very clearly in conversation and feels self-conscious about it. In the process of telling me this, she falters in her speech, shrugs her shoulders, and says, "See? I'm doing it right now."

I ask her to look me in the eyes and say, "It is entirely up to *me* to be sure that you understand what I am saying." After she says that, I ask, "True or false?" She answers, "No, but it would sure help you if I could speak half-decently."

I resist the natural urge to reassure that she talks quite well and that I will work with her. I recognize that her "No, but . . ." translates "True" in answer to my challenge. She still talks only about *her* responsibility for *my* understanding of what she says, seeing herself as totally responsible for the outcome of an inherently co-operative enterprise. With this attitude she indirectly insults others, since it implies that they contribute nothing of consequence to the task of understanding what she thinks and feels. No wonder she often finds her adult kids irritated at her in simple conversations.

I ask this woman what part she thinks others play in the process of comprehending what she means. She pauses, frowns, grins, and slowly says, "Hmm, I guess I've never thought about that."

The question has always eluded her until I make it accessible by having her look at herself through different eyes than she usually does. She habitually limits her perspective by overemphasizing her own portion of the responsibility for what happens in the lives of people relating to her. My challenge opens the door for her to ask other people to work *with* her.

## How to Present Logical Challenges

### Prepare People

The dentists I have liked best over the years have all had one characteristic in common—before they do something that I might feel, they prepare me for it. They say, "I'm going to give you a shot of novocaine now. You'll feel the prick of the needle, then in a couple minutes this whole lower left side of your jaw will be numb enough that I can proceed with drilling." By explaining to me what will happen and why, they free me to cooperate and spare me from the feeling that I have to outguess them or protect myself from what they do.

Using that principle, I employ a variety of sentences to prepare clients for the first logical challenge I offer them. These preparations all have a flavor like this: "I want to be sure I'm correctly following the thought you're expressing. Let me give you a sentence to say, then you tell me if it accurately captures what you think. The sentence is this: '_____.'" More briefly, especially after I've done it once, I ask, "Would it fit for you to say '_____'?" Or I might say, "Try this one on for size: '_____.'"

### Have Them Say It

I offer the challenges for clients to say *aloud*. If they ask me why, I answer something like one of these:

"Just to see how it sounds to you."

"So you can try it on like a suit of clothes and tell me how it fits you."

"I want you to feel the weight of what you're saying and tell me if
  you really mean it when you think about it."

"It's just a lot different to *say* something yourself than to hear it
  said to you."

Occasionally clients say they don't want to repeat my statements, or they don't like having me put words in their mouths. I
reply that we certainly do not *need* to use such a technique, and I
do not want to bulldoze them, but since it is a technique that many
people find helpful, I would like to see how we can adapt it for use
in our work together. If they still refuse, I simply state each challenge and ask, "True or false?" without insisting that they repeat
the sentence(s).

After clients repeat a challenge for themselves and pause a second to let it soak in, I ask, "True or false?" I generally word the first
challenge of a progressive sequence in such a way that the client
will probably answer "True." Then I devise a slightly more extreme
statement of the same idea and offer that as the second challenge
for the client to repeat and declare true or false. I keep escalating
the absurdity and outrageous arrogance of each statement, one
baby step at a time, until the client finally answers "False!" Then I
ask why this one was judged "False" but the one before it "True."
What I am probing for is how the two statements differ in the
client's appraisal.

A well-constructed ladder of challenges proceeds by small-
enough steps of impeccable-enough logic that a client readily sees
each one as a fitting outgrowth of its predecessor. Just as an absurd
conclusion reached by a valid logical process reveals a faulty starting premise, belief systems built upon sand foundations collapse
under the wind and rain of perceptive logical challenges.

### Lead Them to Something Better

I seek not merely to destroy false beliefs, but to institute and
strengthen correct beliefs in their place. So, when clients say
"False" to a challenge, I ask, "What's false about it?" or "What is
true instead?" I thereby get them to articulate beliefs true to the
Word of God that they already hold in fetal form. We enter a kin-
dergarten of theological education.

For example, a client laughs and says "False" to a highly esca-
lated challenge such as: "I am in a position to dictate orders to

Almighty God." When I ask what makes that statement false, the client pauses a moment and answers with refreshing childlike innocence, "Well, if God really is almighty, that means he's the boss of everything. And nobody bosses the boss!" To consolidate such a healthy new belief, in place of the one the client has only temporarily left, I gently ask something like, "Well, if you're not in a position to boss the boss, what position *are* you in?" I am nudging the client toward some such affirmation as: "I'm at his mercy, and he is merciful."

### Do Mostly Informal Challenges

I present less than half my challenges in a formal sequence of logical steps. Most I offer only one at a time, and generally without requiring clients to restate them. I present them as mere extensions of active listening.

I begin empathic listening well within the bounds of what clients consciously tell me. I convey by posture, eye contact, head nodding, and "mhmm" that I am working to understand what clients are communicating to me. I frequently express this effort with something like, "Let me see if I can say that correctly in my words."

Central to all this close listening, I regard myself as an educable retardate (see "Slow It Down," in chapter 1). Actually, I am using a method of persuasion that Socrates made famous. One dictionary refers to "Socratic irony: a pretense of ignorance, though one may be wise, in order to expose the errors of an opponent's reasoning."

Though I need clients to forgive my "slow learning," I expect to get the point with enough repetition, restatement, emphasis, and slowed pace. I normally do not say my disclaimers aloud to clients, lest they view me as mocking them. But thinking of myself this way helps me to maintain a disarming demeanor and neutralize any appearance that I (with my superior tools of advanced psychological training) lie in wait to sadistically detect and expose some ugly foolishness tucked away in a client's mental privacy.

To that end, I frown puzzled looks, scratch my head, and review sentence-by-sentence what a client has just said. I come across a little mentally slow and easily confused, with a let-me-get-this-straight attitude. Then I preface the rapier challenge with words like, "Would another way of saying that be '_____'?" Or, "Would I be accurate in understanding you to say '_____'?" I follow with a trenchant, motto-like logical challenge.

Probably a third of such challenges fail to trigger a recognition reflex. Then I say, "Help me. What am I missing? How does that statement *not* apply to you?" What the client says next helps me to hone my challenge to more accurately fit the dynamics of the situation.

When one of my informal, active-listening challenges does create a significant recognition reflex, I might formalize it by telling the client, "Maybe you had better say that one out loud."

### *Follow-Through*

When challenges take effect in clients, they usually evoke remarks like, "That doesn't make much sense when I hear myself say it, but that *is* the way I think." I might then ask, "What makes *more* sense?" Remember that a good challenge creates a teachable moment. Having just let go of an old belief, clients pause in a cognitive search for a new one. Seldom do counselors find clients more suggestible. How counselors use that golden opportunity grows out of their own morality and beliefs.

Counselors who say nothing imply that one belief is as good as another for a particular client to hold. At the other extreme are counselors who jam in a bunch of doctrine in *their* words, conveying by this action that clients don't have enough brains to arrive at improved beliefs by reasoning through what they already do know. I prefer the middle approach of actively guiding the direction in which the clients will reason. For example, I ask, "What might God say if you consulted him on this topic?" Or, "What Scripture do you know that touches on this matter?" If the answer comes back as "None," I may then inquire, "I wonder if 1 John 1:9 might apply."

Such semi-directiveness reflects a cooperative venture—the counselor suggests areas to explore, while leaving latitude in what a client might discover there. Complete non-directive leadership is impossible in vitality therapy since the very fact that counselors challenge some beliefs shows that they consider other beliefs better to hold. Of course, Christian counselors care about what authority their clients consult in seeking new beliefs. Therefore they do not ask, "Have you consulted the works of Karl Marx?" Nor do they suggest, "Trust your gut feelings."

Sometimes I get more direct at teachable moments, maybe clarifying a point of doctrine, like this: "Have you ever heard the word *sovereign*?" I ask clients what they think the sovereignty of God

*Ag them personally*

means. Then I tell them that they actually stated it quite clearly a moment earlier when they said that nobody else bosses the boss. I might add a thought-provoking idea about sin as the attempt by powerless creatures to oust the Almighty from his position and install themselves as sovereigns over him. Seldom have clients come to that advanced a concept of sin. They typically regard sin as doing naughty things that make important people, such as God, mad at them.

### Keep Them on Track

Having heard me state a challenge for them to repeat, clients sometimes do not actually say it, but instead go off on a tangent that obliquely answers it. For example:

*Counselor:* "I'd like you to say this sentence out loud to see how it fits for you: If God really loved me, he would make everything turn out the way I want it to."

*Client:* "Oh, I know we're not always supposed to get everything we want."

In such cases, I first direct clients to the task at hand by a simple rhetorical question: "Will you say the sentence out loud yourself?" Second, with clients who persist in not doing that simple assignment, I call their attention to that resistance and ask if they intentionally prefer not to do what I am suggesting. Of course, if they clearly state an objection to saying it, I explore their objection before returning to the challenge itself. But most clients simply do not realize that they have talked *about* the challenge instead of slowing down, saying it, feeling its impact on them, and then answering "True" or "False" when requested to do so.

This kind of mental rushing is a bad habit that keeps people from thinking and from hearing the still, small voice of God beckoning: "Be still. Know that I am God. Then come and let us reason together." I take as a central mission this courteously relentless task of slowing down the process and returning clients to the issues they need to soberly ponder.

Sometimes I write out a key challenge and give it to a person to take home from our session. In my office I also routinely tape-record (with client's permission) so that I can give a client the tape of our session to take away and listen to one or more times at home or elsewhere.

# 8

# Miscellaneous Tactics

The logical challenges in the previous chapter aimed to arouse in people responses that *oppose the wording*. This is a provocative technique, closely related to paradoxical interventions—what the general public has long meant by "using a little psychology." What is actually being used is *reverse psychology,* in which you tell people to do something so as to induce them to do the opposite. That perfect governess, Mary Poppins, got two rebellious children to go to sleep when they refused. She wisely agreed with them in her words: "Stay awake; don't sleep and dream." But they amounted to the words of a lullaby that soon allowed benign sleepiness to have its way with the weary young warriors. This adroit playing of devil's advocate is one of several miscellaneous techniques to be presented in this chapter.

## Starting Clearly

### Take Charge

*Set your own attitude.* You may never actually say these words, but the following sentences convey the attitudes that will keep you vital in doing your counseling work: "I really like you, client. What you've got here is not easy. I'm not surprised that you're having trouble with it. Let's see what we can do about it together. I'm sure we can figure something out."

*Define the problem.* Right from the start, get a workable problem statement that is as precise as possible. Ask, "What brings you here?" Or, "What did you want to see me about?" Or, "What's the problem?" Since troubled people often do a remarkably poor job of defining their problems, some of your most rapid and effective counseling can come at this initial stage of problem clarification. Even your rewording of their complaints in different ways than they have done can make them seem less formidable in clients' eyes.

145

Clients frequently announce difficulties that are simply part and parcel of traveling the bumpy road of everyday life. Be ready to ask at such times, "How is that a *problem* for you?" What *you* mean by "problems" are dilemmas to which clients have already applied their full coping abilities only to remain baffled and unsuccessful. They simply do not see some option open to them, or they rule it out for reasons they have not thought to question. You are looking for some kind of "stuckness," not just discomfort.

For example, a man may report his problem as: "I have low self-esteem." By asking how it is a problem for him, you help him to focus on what this condition keeps him from *doing*. These further questions may help him define his problem:

"Are you sure? What makes you *think* you have low self-esteem? How will you know when you don't?"

"What will you be doing when you have better self-esteem that you don't think you can do now?"

"When *have* you had the kind of self-esteem you want?" (If client answers, "Never," ask, "If you don't know what it's like, how will you recognize it when you get it?")

"Suppose that a miracle happens and the problems that bring you here are suddenly solved. How will you know it? How will your wife know it? Who else will know? What will they see and hear that will convince them that you are different?"

"What will be the first faint signs to you that this time with me today has helped you?"

*Ask more about the problem.* Bear in mind that the information you seek and the manner in which you seek it can in itself relieve clients. For example, routinely ask:

"Why are you coming for help on it *now* rather than sooner or later?"

"What was the last straw?"

"What prompted you to contact me about it *at this time*?"

"What happened the hour [or day] before you set this appointment with me?"

These questions can help clients to realize that the main thing fueling their current anguish is a specific incident that precipitated their contact with you. This also subtly reminds them that they *were* adequately handling quite a bit until this particular "last straw."

Similar relief comes from such questions as: "How long has this problem been going on?" "When did it start?" "What else was going on in your life at that time?"

Especially with recent public awareness of the concept of life stresses, people can relate their current distresses to other difficulties that they had not considered connected. For example, a woman complains to you that her husband is withdrawn and "unfriendly" to her. She supposes that he no longer loves her. Upon your asking when this started and what else was happening then, she thinks a moment and answers, "About four months ago, right after his brother died suddenly of a heart attack." Just hearing those two facts mentioned side by side might prompt a flash of insight on her face and a question: "You don't think those two events could be related to each other, do you?" What an entirely different problem statement it is for this wife to say, "My husband is grieving," rather than, "He no longer loves me."

### Assess "Customership"

Three categories of clients will come to you:

*Customers* are people with complaints and the willingness to take actions to resolve their complaints.

*Complainants* are people with complaints but who want someone else to change or the circumstances to modify, in order for them to feel better. They do not see themselves as able or responsible to do anything more than register their grievances. They are stuck temporarily in a tattletale's mentality with regard to the complaint at hand. In primary-school terms, tattletales are kids who consider their entire duty discharged merely upon having reported something out of order to a person in authority. They do not think in terms of rolling up their own sleeves to pitch in and fix the disorder.

*Visitors* are people who consult a counselor because someone else wants them to. At least initially they have no investment in improving things. Here are three classic examples of *visitors:*

A husband is dragged along by his wife, who insists that *he* needs counseling because he won't talk to her. Actually, he is quite content with their current communication level. *She* is not. So she is the one with the problem: "What can *I* do— either to get my husband to talk more with me or to adjust myself to less talking than I would like?" As soon as the wife agrees to that statement of goal for the counseling, she is a customer. As long as she insists that *she* should not have to do anything to get him to talk—that he needs to get over some problem inside him that keeps him from talking with her— she remains a *complainant,* not a *customer.*

Teenagers are sometimes forced to go to a counselor because they are breaking rules their parents have set. Not one in a hundred of these young people will look you in the eye and say, "I really need help. I'm having a hard time getting myself to abide by some rules that my parents want me to follow. Can you please help me to find the inner motivation to obey them as I should?"

Persons may be sentenced by legal authorities to get counseling because of some law they broke. If they come to the counselor only to satisfy the court, they approach counselors with an air of, "Okay, here I am. Go ahead and do your thing on me."

As the counselor, try to convert *visitors* and *complainants* into *customers.* When you are not sure which category a client is in, but you have a vague feeling of his or her non-involvement, ask, "Do you *want* to be here? What for? What will happen if you *don't* meet with me? How will you know when you have gotten what you came here for?" This type of probing may lead you to a workable problem statement, for example—in the case of the criminal—"I want to figure out how to get the court off my back."

You might also ask, "Whose idea was it for you to see me? What did that person hope would result? How interested are *you* in such a result?" When this does not create a *customer,* at least you can do some beneficial work on the *visitor's* attitude toward the person who sent him or her to you. You dignify clients by assigning them the role of consultants to you regarding the senders. Ask teenagers, for example, "What is going on with your parents that they feel so urgent about having you come to see me?" Then seek to arouse compassion (in place of resentment) in the teens by speculating that these poor folks, the parents, must be quite fearful that people will think they are uncaring about their youngsters. "Or perhaps your parents worry that you don't love them?" you might wonder aloud.

This clarification of "customership" can save you some frustrating involvements in family situations where everyone volunteers one member as the sick one. Let's say there is an unemployed adult son living with Mom and Dad after a couple of hospitalizations for mental problems. Since this son acts obviously inadequate, you probably find it easy to regard him as "the needy patient." But suppose he comes to counseling with no goals for personal change, with only vague self-criticisms at best, such as: "I really should get my act together." The son comes as a *visitor*—simply because other family members think he drains Mom and Dad too much. Find the *customer* by asking such questions as these:

"Who is most bothered by John's problems?"

"Who is second most bothered?"

"Who will be happiest when John improves?

"Do these persons want my help in learning how to handle the difficulties that John creates for *them*?"

"If John improves, what will these persons be able to do that they do not think they can do now?"

Further encourage someone to become a *customer* by a statement like, "I am amazed that Mom and Dad would put themselves at John's mercy by thinking that the only way they can be comfortable is for *him* to change."

### Keep Control

Much like children, people who come to you in emotional distress need firm limits in order to feel secure. They need assurance that *you* know how to set and enforce rules that will make their consultations with you more productive than their own hysterical gropings. They need to see you maintain consistent, firm discipline of both the situation and your own emotions, so that being "firm" means you do not become harsh or lose patience, no matter how much people test you.

*Consistently refocus*. In crises, clients often present themselves with poor self-control of their own thinking processes. They need you to lay down railroad tracks for them to ride on and to keep them from sidetracking on the journey. Sidetracking represents the primary way that confused individuals or conflictual partners interfere with their own orderly problem solving. It occurs by changing the focus of conversation from the topic that had been on the floor to another, without negotiating the change by mutual agreement.

Let's consider an example of sidetracking by a conflictual husband (H) and wife (W) and how the counselor (CO) repeatedly refocuses as necessary:

CO: So you two want my help in resolving the clash you've had over his forgetting her birthday. Right?

W: Yes, he *always* forgets important dates. It's because he doesn't care about anybody but himself. He never—

H: You're no one to talk. You keep the house looking like a pig pen and—

CO: Hold it! Hold it! Let's get back to the question of how to heal the hurt about the birthday. What have you tried so far?

W: Well, I told him how much it hurt me.

CO: Then what happened?

W: Oh, what's the use? Why even bother? Look at him sitting over there so smug and proud of himself.

CO: Hold it! What happened next after you told your husband that you felt hurt when he forgot your birthday?

H: That's not the way she said it. She lit into me like a gored ox. Why she—

CO: Wait a minute! I want to know what happened next after she showed her hurt. You, husband, what do you remember?

H: All I remember is that she attacked me because she *wanted* to hurt me, because she's nothing but a vicious witch! You can ask anybody who knows her. They all think she's a witch.

W: Who does? You just name one person. They all think you—

CO: Stop! Whoa! Hold it!

W: But he always—

CO: Hold it! Hang on! We need to have a ground rule here. One person speaks at a time, and *on* the topic we are discussing. Right now that topic is what happened next after she made it known that she felt hurt when he forgot her birthday. Wife, what happened next, the way *you* remember it?

w: Well, I think he just threw up his hands, as if *he* were the one more hurt than I.

co: You know, maybe it wasn't that one of you felt hurt and the other didn't. It sounds to me as though you *both* felt hurt and still do.

h: I don't know where all this is getting us. She's got her pea-sized brain made up, and nothing's ever going to change it.

co: Another ground rule: no name-calling. It doesn't help, and it gets you both off the topic. No wonder you're so frustrated in your talks.

h: Hey, what makes *you* think you can tell *me* what to do? Just because you're some kind of hot-shot expert or something doesn't make you better than me.

co: Let me paint a picture for you, folks. I'm kind of like a dentist. I need you to help me, in order for me to help you. The ground rules I'm setting are absolutely essential for the two of you to observe if you are going to benefit from your time with me. My job is to see to it that the two of you work together in an orderly, respectful fashion to solve the problems that are coming between you. Now let me address a new question to you, wife. Why do you suppose your husband felt hurt when you reminded him that he forgot your birthday?

*Assert your leadership.* Near the end of the above dialogue, the husband not only broke the rule against sidetracking, but challenged the counselor's right to set rules. This required the counselor to go beyond refocusing into a more global assumption of the role of director, master of ceremonies, or parliamentarian. Without saying it, the counselor put before the couple (note, not *just* the husband) the implied ultimatum: "Work with me, or I won't meet with you." To state this policy another way: "Do things the way I say to, or I won't know how to apply my skills to your situation, and there won't be any point in our meeting."

This policy and the need for boldness-with-courtesy in applying it come into play particularly with on-and-on talkers. They want to fill you in on gallons of background information that will drown you into sleepy overload if you dutifully listen to it in order not to offend them. Like tattletales, they think they are doing you a favor to give you all the details they know. You know better. You know that therapeutic results are going to come from how you direct the inquiry, not from the volume of data reported or even its accuracy. Rehearsing the familiar once again only keeps nervous talkers stuck with it. You must stop them firmly without bruising them. Here's an example of how a counselor (CO) might assert his or her leadership with a client (CL):

CO: What brings you to see me?

CL: Well, first of all let me give you some background. I was born the fifth of six children. My mother died when I was three. My father drank all the time and I only saw him sober two, no maybe three, no it was only two times—I remember because we lived in Charlotte at the time—that was just before we moved to Rangoon, which was where my father almost married a Viennese woman named—let's see what was her name? No, no, don't interrupt me. I'll get it. She had black hair and—

CO: Excuse me a moment. The background is important, and I do want to hear it, but first I need some particular information from you in order for me to make sense of what you tell me. What problem do you want my help with?

CL: Oh, but this will only take a minute, and it is *so* important. You see, my grandfather on my mother's side had scurvy as a boy—that was in Arkansas—and so he—

CO: Pardon me for interrupting, but I need to ask you a couple of questions before we go further with your background. What are you hoping will be the result of your coming to see me?

CL: I just have to tell you this part first. My oldest brother converted to Buddhism in 1949 and almost died, but now he and I are very close. Anyway, he married a girl who—

CO: I have to stop you again. This is the third time I have told you that I must know where you are headed before I know how to make use of the background you give me. Humor me. Give me a preview of coming attractions before the main feature. What do you want to get out of my help?

CL: I'll tell you just as soon as I finish the history.

CO: First tell me what you want from counseling.

CL: I'm just telling you that my family had a lot of mental illness in it, especially on my father's side—brother, you should know my Uncle Nero. Why, he—

CO: Hang on a minute! I really need to know what you hope to gain from seeing me.

CL: Just let me finish this part.

CO: First tell me what you want from counseling.

CL: Now take Harry, my half-breed hairdresser—

CO: [again interrupting] I need to know what you want from counseling.

CL: I only want to add one more item.

CO: You know, I'm kind of surprised that you ignore my directions after you have gone to considerable trouble to arrange this time to meet me. Was it *your* idea to come here?

CL: Yes!

CO: What for?

CL: Well, you see, in 1965—

CO: [interrupting!] Hold it. You're still ignoring me. If you don't tell me *now* why you are coming to see me, I will end this conversation and not schedule another one with you until you show me in writing what you want my help with.

CL: Uh—well—you see—I've just been told I have cancer, and I don't know what to do.

### Later-Session Start-Ups

When beginning a follow-up session, do not ask general, chatty questions that give clients a blank check with which to orient the new meeting toward the negative. Ask things that invite them to report their positive observations and successful actions pertaining to the things you talked about last time. Instead of, "How are you doing?" or "What's new?" or "What do you want to talk about today?" ask something like, "What have been the first signs you noticed that things might be improving a little?"

Suppose you had given a binge-eater this homework assignment: "Between now and next time we talk, notice what you do when you *overcome* the urge to binge." Then you ask at the start of your next talk, "What did you notice that you do when you overcome the urge to binge?"

By this kind of question, you convey your expectation that clients take counseling seriously as *theirs,* and that they work between meetings with you as well as during them.

## Tilting Toward Health

### Use Presuppositional Wording

You can select the phrasing of your questions and comments in ways that cast your clients and their future situations in an optimistic, encouraging light. For example:

1. "How will you and I know when this counseling has been successful?" This wording embeds the unspoken implication within it that this counseling *will* succeed. It's only a question of time— "when," not "if."

2. "Tell me about some times when this problem arose, but it didn't bother you much." This request gives the message that all difficulties vary in their intensity from time to time. Therefore, it pays us to notice the differences to see what makes thing better, at least some of the time. Knowing that, we can probably figure out some ways to influence events more in the preferable direction. It also suggests the idea of eliminating many complaints from the "problem" category simply by choosing to tolerate them. That becomes a particularly sensible way, for example, to handle the irritations caused by an elderly loved one's mannerisms of forgetfulness, crankiness, or eccentric demands.

3. "What was different about times when the problem happened but it turned out for the better?" This question re-orients clients from "either/or" thinking to "both/and." That is, besides the outcomes that they did *not* like, what else happened that on balance made the whole unsought experience worthwhile? This viewpoint affords much more liberty than the usual constricted perspective brought by clients when seeking help—that things have got to become totally the way they want them to be.

### Future Orientation

Just getting clients talking about how the future will look without the problem tends to foster resolution. Consider the case of a businessman who fears flying and asks your help to get over this phobia enough to make a trip scheduled for the following month. You say, "Help me build a picture of what you're looking for. I mean, what will you consider a successful trip? Let's suppose you've landed at your destination, for example. Where will you go first, to the baggage claim or the car-rental desk?"

The man talks about that for a while, including such details as what model and size of car he will rent. Then you ask similar details about where he will stay, when he will call his wife, what he will say, how he will brag, what she will say, how he will celebrate his success, and so on. All of this serves to settle in his mind that he *is* going to do it. The enjoyable rehearsed activities at the destination begin to become attractive enough to him to outweigh his dislike for the process necessary to get there.

If, instead of this future orientation, you let the client lead the conversation into a focus on his fear, you inadvertently help him to rehearse avoidance. So, you steer away from his original question, "How am I going to get over this terror?" Substitute something like, "When you're through this episode, how do you *want* to be able to say you did it?"

### Avoid Negative Predictions

I occasionally hear negative reports from clients about consultations they had years earlier with other mental-health professionals who meant well but who unwisely planted seeds of unhealthy actions. In one such case, a Christian therapist had told a young man, "The way you are going, I see an affair and a divorce ahead of you." The man later came to me during the affair that *did* occur, and in the midst of divorce proceedings that his wife did not want. His motivation to rebuild his marriage was seriously eroded by the earlier therapist's prediction, which the man took virtually as permission, since an expert had presented it as inevitable.

In the above case, if I had been the therapist who met years ago with the young husband, I would have said something more like, "You know, I see in you the character qualities to turn even frustrating dry spells and gut-wrenching conflicts into solid steps forward for both your marriage and your growth as a man of God."

That course, rather than the "dire predictions" method, seems to me what is indicated by the inspiring Scripture in Hebrews 10:24:

"And let us consider *and* give attentive, continuous care to watching over one another, studying how we may stir up (stimulate and incite) to love *and* helpful deeds *and* noble activities" (AMPLIFIED).

### Ask Questions Likely to Get "Yes" Answers

When I meet with troubled married couples for the first time, I generally ask (partway through the meeting), "Do you *want* to stay married to each other?" If they each answer *yes,* it gives a profound boost to the mood of all our subsequent times together. With that affirmative reply, they seem to have broken some barrier and set themselves on course toward a positive outcome. I see it as a mini-renewal of their wedding vows.

Even if a partner answers, "I'm not sure," it seems to break that person's own heart a little and thereby create a slight bend toward reconciliation. Even an outright "No" clears the air, at least enough to free that person from a sense of entrapment in the marriage.

### Ask for a No-Suicide Decision

I regularly ask all my clients in our first session if they have had any suicidal thoughts. Then I ask them if they will agree to rule out the possibility of acting on any such thoughts. I do not play around with asking why they might want to do it. Neither do I try to talk them out of it nor invite them to call me at any hour of day or night if they feel suicidal. I simply ask them if they will make a decision for themselves, not a promise to me, that they will never take their own lives. I extend the same approach to pull the fuses out of any other time bombs ticking in their lives, such as killing someone else, punching someone out, impulsively quitting a job or telling off the boss, having a nervous breakdown, filing for divorce, or running away.

I pretty much do it the same way with every client. Toward the end of our time together I say, "Very often, when people decide to contact a counselor, it's at a time when they are at such a low that they aren't sure they even want to live any more. Have you had any thoughts like that?" Probably one-third to one-half of the people I ask this say *yes.*

I then ask if they have had any thoughts of ending their own lives. Most say a clear *no* or that the thought may have crossed their minds but they don't think they would have the courage to do it, or some such reason. I then ask if they have yet made a firm decision *not* to take their own lives, no matter what. If they do not say *yes,* I ask if they will consider making such a decision right now. When they agree to that suggestion, I say:

> Let me give you a way to do it. I will say the sentence, then you say it out loud after me, then you tell me if it expresses *your* decision. The sentence is this: "I will never take my own life, either accidentally or on purpose, no matter what." Okay? Now you say it.

After the clients say it (or the same idea in other words), I pause and then ask, "True or false?" or "Is that a decision for you?" Once they affirm it, I go on to ask what they will do instead of killing themselves if they feel desperate and start thinking of suicide. Most answer that they will contact some helping person.

With people who refuse to make the no-suicide decision anywhere along this line, I pursue it in several ways. I might ask, "What's your objection to such a decision?" I ask them what it does *for* them to keep open the option of killing themselves, and also what it *costs* them. If they seem fairly serious about suicide, especially if their thoughts have a lot of such vengeful components as: "They'll finally miss me when I'm gone," I contaminate their fantasies about it. For example, I ask who will discover the body and what that person will say. Will their children say, "Oh, boy, what a relief to have that old drag of a parent out of my life"? I might be very specific: "Will the corpse's eyes be open or closed? Will it probably lose its bowel and bladder contents before the wagon arrives to haul it away?" I want these fantasies unglamorous, both to remove any fantasies of control over others and to marshal people's own pride *against* suicide.

I don't get into power struggles by pleading with clients to make the decision. Of course, if someone in conversation with me convincingly threatened to end it all immediately, I would contact the police, as would any citizen. But with people who just want to hold open the possibility of killing themselves sometime, I end the discussion with them this way:

> Well, I can't make the decision for you. That's one area where *you* are sovereign. Even God won't stop you. Only you can decide to keep yourself alive. I hope you won't kill yourself, but I can't stop you. I just have one thing to say to you about it: "DON'T kill yourself!"

I state that last command as forcefully as I can, as if I am literally injecting a lifesaving serum into their arteries. I want an indelible image of my face and voice saying "DON'T!" to arise in their memories at any future time they stand at the point of suicide.

The part about "accidentally or on purpose" in the no-suicide sentence aims to close loopholes, such as when a depressed man lets himself fall asleep at the wheel of his car and have a suicide by carelessness, which renders him just as dead as a premeditated act. The accident clause adds to the seriousness of the decision statement, in that it anticipates apparent compliances that mask attempts to get around it.

### Explore Exceptions and Past Successes

Having a crisis tends to give clients tunnel vision. They focus so intently on what bothers them that they overlook the occasions when it does *not* occur. For example, parents asking for help to cure a child's bedwetting seldom give any thought to those nights when the bed is dry. To identify successes in that situation, as counselor you can ask questions like, "How many nights a week does your child wet the bed? What is different about the nights when the bed is *dry?*"

Such questions may help the parents discover that their boy wets on the nights that Mom puts him to bed, but not when Dad does. *Solution:* Have Dad put the boy to bed. These parents already had a way to solve their problem but just did not realize it.

Similarly, many people have already met and solved problems quite like the one they now face, but they simply do not think to apply again what worked before. For example, a young couple moves into a new house and soon complains to you of water on their basement floor every time it rains very hard. You ask them how flooding problems were prevented in the homes in which they grew up. One answers, "We never had to deal with that because we lived in a low area where all the homes had sump pumps in the basements to keep them dry." You muse, "I wonder what a sump pump might do for your present situation." They try it and it works—and they consider you a genius! Actually, you only brought one brilliant idea into their lives: the recognition that they already knew how to solve their problem.

Make it a regular practice to ask this straightforward question: "Have you ever faced a similar difficulty before? How did you handle that one?" More specifically, with couples who complain to you that they fight all the time, ask, "How do your fights *end?*" Or, for someone who reports a bad habit involving loss of self-control, ask, "Tell me about some times when you felt the urge to indulge your habit, but did not."

## Taking a Think Break

Suppose you meet with a client for about an hour. Ten minutes before you end the session, excuse yourself for five minutes to go into another room. Tell the person that you want to think over what the two of you have been talking about and then come back with some conclusions and recommendations. When you return after this "think break," you spend your last five minutes with the person—sharing those thoughts and also making plans together for your next meeting or follow-up.

Those five minutes away usually create a remarkable effect on clients. When you return they receive you with unusual attentiveness, which reflects a mixture of curiosity and awe. Somehow you take on the aura of an expert by having gone away to contemplate the issues at hand. You show that you take the hour's conversation seriously by applying your concentrated efforts to preparing a summary and suggestions. Clients know they will take something home from their time with you. This procedure also decreases their tendency to ask doorknob questions, partly because you give them an "assignment," but even more because you let them know what you think of them. It satisfies a kind of closure hunger that hovers over the end of most counseling interviews.

During your five-minute break, summarize to yourself your thoughts and feelings about the client and the time you have just spent together. Concentrate particularly on coming up with three to five feedback statements that you will present as compliments. A summary in this positive vein will accomplish four things:

1. Sweeten your own attitude toward the client
2. Reduce the client's fear of criticism from you
3. Let the client know that you have heard his or her central message to you
4. Create hopeful momentum for change by establishing that the client is already doing something right

Also design recommendations during your break, ideas that

build on the positive momentum created by your compliments. They will give clients something to do in preparation for your next meeting (or something to chew on if you never meet again). As a prescription, you can often tell a client to do whatever you have learned he or she is already doing that makes things better. Such ideas come out of exploring "exceptions" to the problem (as previously discussed in this chapter). You can get further ideas from asking clients what they will be doing when their problems are solved. Then simply prescribe some of those "future" actions for them to begin doing now. For instance, a depressed man tells you that he will probably spend a day at the seashore when he no longer feels depressed. You assign him to spend a day at the seashore as a kind of research project, to see what in particular he likes about the experience. He thinks that enjoyable activities have to wait until he feels ready to enjoy them. You know—but don't tell him—that doing the enjoyable activities can create the feelings of enjoyment.

### Homework Assignments

A few generic prescriptions work wonders in almost every situation, independent of the nature of problems people bring to you. I have borrowed the following from Michelle Weiner-Davis's excellent workshops on Solution-Focused Brief Therapy (1988). Give clients one of the following assignments at the end of your time together, right after your compliments.

*The Inventory Task.* "We have talked today mostly about things that are distressing you, that you want to change. What I'd like you to do between now and next time is take an inventory of what is already going on in your life that you want to be sure continues as it is."

*The Pits Task.* "After you leave here today I'd like you to decide if you have probably hit bottom already. In other words, ask yourself if this is the pits—as bad as it's likely to get—or if things will probably have to get still worse *before* they start to get better."

*The Surprise Task.* (This is used when you counsel two persons related to each other.) "Between now and next time we meet, do one or two things to surprise your partner [or parent, child, etc.] but don't talk about what it is. Keep it a secret until you get here. Then I will ask each of you to guess what the other person did to surprise you. So watch like a hawk to see what it might be!"

*The Self-Control Task.* "Notice what you do when you *overcome* the temptation to indulge your habit."

*The Noticing-Health Task.* "Notice what is different about the days that are better than others; then account for the differences."

In a way, all the above prescriptions orient clients to *notice* what is going well rather than what is discouraging. Just having put them into an attitude of awareness changes their whole way of participating in problem situations. Entering deliberately as an alert observer breaks up the automatic quality of spontaneous troubles that clients believe they "can't do anything about. The Pits Task works especially well with strongly hopeless complainers. It agrees with them that things are terrible, and even preempts their future complaints by saying that things could get worse yet. But it embeds the notion that the worst is a way station to the better. The Surprise Task redirects the vigilance of loved ones at odds with each other. They normally watch for anything the other parties do that offers further proof against them. This new task motivates them to notice what a loved one does that is affectionate, kind, and cooperative with the purposes of counseling.

Sometimes you can have self-starting clients design their own assignments by asking, "What do you want to be ready to report to me next time?" They may thrive under just knowing that they are going to be accountable to someone else for reaching their own goals.

### Giving Compliments

Your first words need to be positive when you return to clients from your think break. They are braced for the worst, fearing that you are going to fault them for the troubles they are in, or for not having solved them sooner, or for being selfish or weak or foolish. So you begin each compliment with such words as these:

"I am impressed that . . ."

"I was struck that . . ."

"It really moved me that . . ."

"It really comes through strongly that . . ."

Then add some conclusions such as these:

". . . you showed a lot of courage in coming for counseling."

". . . you've already begun moving in the right direction."

". . . you're doing amazingly well under very difficult circumstances. You must be doing *something* right!"

". . . you care very deeply about the things we have talked about." (This is particularly appropriate if the person came near tears at some point.)

". . . your partner's goodwill *really* matters to you." (This is helpful if loved ones viciously accuse each other of unloving actions or neglect.)

## Confronting the Tough Ones

### *Examples of Tough Cases*

Some difficult kinds of persons can be baffling. They demand an inordinate amount of your time and energy as a counselor, only to show dissatisfaction with what you have done and unrelieved desperation about their chronic problems. Such clients come to you with urgent anguish about problems that have hung over their heads for a long time but that they need to resolve *now.* They portray themselves as helpless and their destiny as entirely up to you.

Example 1: A woman comes to you twenty minutes late for a fifty-minute time slot you offered her. She announces that she has an urgent decision to make tomorrow morning about a job offer. She has already gotten several opinions from other friends and counselors, some that she should say *yes,* some that she should say *no.* She's running out of time and insists you've got to help her know today which answer is really the right one.

Example 2: A man you have met once before says partway through your second conversation, "I might as well quit talking to you right now. I know you're not interested in what I have to say. This always happens to me. I ruin every friendship I ever start." And he starts to leave.

Example 3: A young woman meeting with you as a client for the first time giggles, squirms in her chair, sighs, looks up at the ceiling, and says, "I feel so nervous here. Do you see a lot of crazy people? Do you think I'm crazy? You do. I'm sure you do. Or else why would I even be asking the question, right? Now I've probably upset you. Have I? I talk too much. You're mad at me, aren't you?"

### *"Borderline" personality disorder.*

Dr. James Masterson, in a series of books including *Psychotherapy of the Borderline Adult* (1976), has described the kinds of patients who present themselves in the unstable, demanding ways illustrated above. The term *borderline* is a misleading one, since it does *not* refer here to a condition that teeters precariously between sanity and psychosis. The scholars who continually refine psychiatric terminology will probably soon offer a more precise label for this predictable cluster of baffling behaviors.

Accusations from these difficult clients have more to do with *them* than with you, even though you feel impotent, furious, and at the same time guilty for having failed these needy people. Masterson teaches long-term psychotherapy for these badly disabled persons. But this chapter will present the best things you can do, when limited to brief encounters with such persons, to preserve your own sanity while benefitting them as much as the situation allows.

### What You Can Do

*Compliment them and give hints.* To the giggly client in Example 3 above, I might say, "Why, of course you're nervous. You hardly know me, yet here you are going to talk about matters deeply private and important to you. You've shown a lot of courage in just coming. So, what do you hope to gain from this time that will make it worth your while to have come?"

Here's another example of how compliments can help: A man who works for his father regularly complies with demands from Dad that he considers unreasonable. Then he balances the resentment he feels by complaining about the situation to other people, now including you. Since he does not explore what he can do differently and his complaining does not improve his situation, you recognize that he comes to you as a complainant, not a customer. You compliment him on being extraordinarily considerate toward his father, especially because he agrees to do things he prefers not to do. You remark that most men in his situation have occasional disagreements with their fathers that help clear the air and establish more equally shared responsibilities in the business (that's a hint!). To his credit, you might elaborate, he shows the manly ability to restrain his sense of injustice and show deference to Dad (another compliment that sandwiches a hint about how he might solve his complaint).

Offering more direct advice to clients of this type tends to produce two bad results:

A     They answer "Yes, but . . ."—telling you why your suggestion
       will not work, and deepening their conviction that you do not
       appreciate the magnitude of the obstacles they face.

B     They get hooked on the special attention they get from you in
       your gifts of advice. They take them as proofs of your love, not
       as tools for them to put to use.

*Set and enforce firm rules.* Panicky and discouraged clients need
structure from you as counselor just as children require from the
adult in charge of any situation. To feel secure, they test you so that
they can find out, to their satisfaction, whether you know what
you're doing enough to keep control of the situation without reject-
ing them, no matter how much they try to take control from you
and recruit you into obeying them.

Accordingly, you state the guiding principle for your counseling
conversations: "You are here to set clear goals for something that
*you* want to accomplish. You must tell what you have tried already,
seriously study why that didn't solve the problem, and think with
me over some new possibilities." Setting this rule lays a foundation
that allows you to confront several typical deviations, such as clients who:

Personally attack you

Take a helpless "I can't" attitude and leave you with total respon-
       sibility to come up with solutions for them

Let "I don't know" stand as their final answer to a problem

Ask (or tell you) how you feel toward them, as in ("You're mad at
       me, aren't you?")

Threaten to leave you, kill themselves, give up on solving the
       problem

Criticize themselves hopelessly

Fall silent and refuse to speak

You enforce the basic rule by immediately pointing out when
clients break it:

"You're not here to talk about me."

"You're tossing the ball to me. What do *you* think?"

Are you going to let 'I don't know' stand as your final answer?"

"How is this behavior helping you?" (in response to threats or self-criticism or silence)

When a client persists in violating the rule, you increase the severity of your confrontation by saying emphatically, "You're doing it *again*! You're *still* doing it!"

With continued violations on their part, you further escalate the intensity of your enforcement by expressing astonishment:

"I'm astonished that you persist in tossing the ball to me when *you* are the one being hurt by the problem."

"I am surprised that you repeatedly turn the focus of our conversation to *my* feelings."

"It amazes me that you settle so easily for 'I don't know.'"

"You seem *determined* to avoid talking about this."

"It is incredible to me how much energy you put into trying to prove your problem can't be solved, instead of into solving it."

You persist as long and emphatically as necessary with the above modes of confrontation until the clients who are testing your resolve either give in and abide by the rule or physically leave your presence. What you are doing is simply holding firm in saying "NO!" to attempts to enlist your complicity in *their* hopelessness.

*Confront non-customers.* Clients who come as complainants often persist in that stuck role simply because they rely too much on one strategy for solving problems. That is, they put all their faith in their ability to coerce *other* people into solving their problems for them. Without realizing it, they concentrate their creative energies on nagging, pressuring, intimidating, inducing guilt, or other manipulative tactics, instead of thinking up things that they themselves can do to make things better.

The following vignette demonstrates how you can point this out to them, and sidestep their attempts to get *you* to do their thinking for them. In this case, the counselor (co) confronts a client (cl) who has been complaining loudly and persistently with angry tears that her husband fails to do enough considerate things for her.

co: I am astonished that you put yourself at your husband's

mercy by clinging to the belief that you can only feel comfort-able when *he* changes.

CL: Okay, then I'll just leave him. That way I won't be at his mercy and I can just take care of myself.

CO: You seem to think that's the *only* possible action you can take.

CL: Well, what else *can* I do?

CO: [Realizes that the client has not just now expressed a bona fide interest in making changes, but has dared the counselor to think for her and let her shoot it all down. She still believes that other people have to change in order for her to feel better. So the counselor works to arouse the wife's own motivation to make things better.] There's really a more important question that comes first, before you can figure out *what* you can do. First tell me *why* you might consider doing anything yourself to make things better, instead of continuing to concentrate your efforts on getting your husband to change so that you feel better.

### *Your Phone-Call Policy*

You need another emphatic rule to protect yourself against the poor self-control that difficult clients generally have. That rule covers your availability by telephone. Your phone policy should be this: "I take unscheduled phone calls only to handle business mat-ters, such as a change of appointment. *I do counseling only at scheduled times.*" Tough clients will test your consistency on this phone policy by calling at unscheduled times, pleading that they have an overwhelming crisis that they can't possibly solve alone and nobody else but you cares enough to help them. With this they threaten indirectly to consign you to the ranks of the uncaring if you do not help them now.

To enforce this rule, you steadfastly refuse to talk (during un-scheduled calls) about the problems that such clients demand you address. Instead, you confront their desperation, their pleas of helplessness, their insistence that they have to have an answer right away. You remind them of their responsibility between meet-ings to think as best they can, to learn by trial and error, to make mental or written notes about what happens with each thing they try, and to thus prepare to make productive use of the next appoint-ment with you. Meanwhile, they are also responsible to develop a network of friends as resource persons when they feel lonely or need comfort in heartbreaking situations. You as counselor must not be too easy a one for them to use in that way. If you give in to their demands, you handicap them from developing the social skills they need.

Keep the calls brief. First ask, "Is this a business call?" When they express urgent desperation, you confront with astonishment as you point out their pattern. For example, "I am amazed that you are calling me about what to do instead of giving it your best shot and telling me about it when we meet next." Suppose the client threatens not to have another time with you. Again you confront: "You seem determined to get me to solve your problem for you. The answer is *no*. We can talk about it next time we meet."

You pause at this point to give clients a chance to successfully do the orderly thing, that is (1) say that they will see you at the next scheduled meeting; and (2) tell you goodbye until then. If instead they press again, you simply repeat, "We can talk about it next time." Then, without further delay or apology, you simply say goodbye and hang up. If the phone rings again immediately, take it off the hook without answering, unplug it and let it sit "busy" for the next hour.

### *Answering Sticky Questions*

People with the tendencies that Masterson lumps into the "borderline" syndrome have an uncanny ability to ask questions with the suction power of a giant squid's tentacles. They almost force you to answer on *their* terms and often increase the questioning's pressure by timing it for the end of a session. With a hand on the doorknob, a difficult client may ask something that you can hardly refuse to answer without seeming rude, stupid, or cowardly. Yet to answer at all puts the control of the counseling's timing and agenda in the client's hands rather than yours. The purpose of these queries lies not in the information they seek, but in letting the client see if he or she can deter you from your stated policies. All such "doorknob questions" translate into one: "Which of us is in charge of what we talk about and when we do it?"

Here follows a list of sticky questions and—in italics—a workable confrontive response to each:

1. "Do you think you can help me? Are we getting anywhere? Are you making sense out of all this?" *I am surprised that you ask my opinion instead of reporting your own.*

2. "Am I crazy? Do you like me? Are you mad at me? Have I been a bad father?" *You seem more concerned with what I think and feel than with what you think and feel.*

3. "Do they have much of a waiting list at the local mental hospital?" *It sounds like you are asking my consent for you to go into a hospital instead of continuing to solve your problems.*

4. "I know we're out of time, but can't you just tell me what I have to do to get my husband to stop his affair?" *That's too serious a question for a quick answer. We don't have time today. We can talk about it next time.*

5. [Desperately] "But what am I going to *do* before next time?" *You're twisting my arm to get me to extend our session. But our time is up for today and we can talk next time about what you tried and what you learned from it.*

6. "Do you believe the Second Coming could come this year? Are you a born-again, Spirit-filled Fundamentalist Christian? Should baptism be by sprinkling?" (Or some other religious question hard to resist answering "Yes" or "No"—but which to answer either way throws you into one side of a controversy that invites clients to talk longer with you or to discredit you for your opinion.) *I wish we had time for more discussion today, but our time is up. We can talk about it next time.*

The following dialogue is a series of questions that challenges your firmness:

"Can't you just answer 'Yes' or 'No'?" *Next time.*

"You mean you're not going to answer me?" *Next time.*

"Just answer me 'Yes' or 'No.'" *Our time is up for today.*

"I won't leave until you answer me." *If you don't leave by yourself, you force me to call the police to remove you.*

### What If They Quit?

Counselors have feelings, too, and many got their primary training in the school of hard knocks, perhaps a rocky childhood situation marked by lots of painful rejection. To have clients turn a cold shoulder when they can't have their way may trigger some of those old painful reactions inside their counselors. Fear of this pain hinders many counselors from exercising the firm control that the most difficult clients require.

What can you—the counselor—do about your own fear? First of all, ask yourself just how eager you are to continue seeing the particular client who threatens to leave you. Generally these intimidators drain so much of your time and attention that you feel relieved when they leave and thus stop harassing you. Second, consider whether you may have something better to do with your time than try to stay in favor with fickle people! Third, take comfort in knowing that you, by holding firm, have shown yourself to be perhaps the most reliable person in that client's life. When he or she finally gets serious about solving problems instead of using them to manipulate others into emotional involvement, you can expect to get a call asking for counseling according to your sound rules.

Take this motto: WHEN YOU CAN'T SERVE, CON-SERVE.

## Recommending Other Resources

### Books and Tapes

Some of the most rapid, effective, and longlasting therapeutic impacts come into clients' lives through books they read. There are several outstanding ones that I recommend, dealing with such topics as child discipline, marital communication, assertiveness, Christian growth, and interpersonal relations. Since some of these books are not readily available in local bookstores or libraries, I keep a supply of them on hand to lend or sell to clients.

When I lend books, I collect a deposit equal to what the book cost me and refund the deposit when the book is returned. Over half of these "lent" books become sales by default when the persons never return them. This policy saves me the friction I used to get into by zealously lending books or tapes to people who promised to return them within a week and never did.

### Seminars, Retreats, Radio and TV Programs

Some people experience remarkable turnarounds in their lives from attending one or more of the excellent programs put on by either local or nationwide ministries. Many church groups have adapted the original Roman Catholic Marriage Encounter format for their own use, with excellent benefit to already-strong marriages. After my wife and I had a rewarding experience with such a weekend in the late 1970s, I immediately had ten of the couples I was counseling sign up. Eight of them had good experiences. The two who did not had gone with the attitude of looking for faults in their partners. They needed preparation in counseling to get them to the point where the weekend experience could do even more for them than counseling could.

### Refer Certain Cases

*To a counselor of the other gender.* If you are a female counselor, don't meet with male clients who want to talk about their sexual fantasies or who have a history of difficulty with impulse control. Similarly, if you are a male counselor, you do best not to work alone with female clients for whom sexual matters are a big focus, either because they themselves are seductive or because they have been the victims of sexual exploitation. If you are a pastor who makes house calls, take your spouse or an elder with you when visiting a parishioner and/or client of the opposite sex.

*To a physician.* Always ask about the physical health of clients who show any symptoms of chronic pain, fatigue, dizziness, heart irregularities—the list could go on. The point is to determine if they are under a medical doctor's care or have recently consulted one about the symptom. Ask, "When did you go? What did you learn? Were you satisfied that the consultation was thorough enough?" Be ready to urge them to see a physician, perhaps a specialist whom you recommend. Have clients call right then for an appointment if you have any suspicion that they won't follow through.

Since many of the above symptoms can come from anxiety or depression, you might get the person recommended back to you by a physician who says there is no physical disorder, just an emotional upset. Nevertheless, to catch the small percentage of cases that are due to hormonal imbalance, a growing tumor in the brain, a persistent infection, or some other organic factor, it makes sense to be scrupulously thorough in regard to medical possibilities.

*To a psychiatrist.* Although psychiatrists are medical doctors who do much of what you do when you counsel, they also have the necessary expertise and legal authority to prescribe medications, to supervise hospitalizations for serious mental disorders, and to administer extreme treatments such as electroshock therapy, which in many cases brings marvelous relief to seriously depressed patients. Have available for consultation one or more psychiatrists whom you trust, either for their advice or to whom you can refer clients (or their family members) when clients seem so out of touch with reality that you cannot get them to respond to you or to put together an intelligible sentence. Keep in mind that most state laws follow as their guideline for hospitalization: "Is the person likely to harm self or others?"

*To self-help groups.* Persons afflicted with compulsive disorders such as substance abuse, sexual addiction, homosexuality, uncontrolled gambling, and the like can generally benefit most from self-help groups of fellow addicts. Alcoholics Anonymous did the pioneering work in this area, with their sound Twelve-Step Program for sobriety through spiritual growth. Many addictions so closely follow stages similar to those of alcoholism that other groups have borrowed AA's ideas and adapted them to different addictions. Sexaholics Anonymous, for example, is one such self-help group. It deals with persons whose lives are significantly hampered by lust, whether just privately acted out or as the focus of such criminal behavior as exhibitionism. Most of these groups have spawned related organizations to assist family members of the addicts. Al Anon is the prototype of these valuable sources of support and wisdom.

Arrange to visit open meetings of one or more of these groups so you know how they function. Have phone numbers available to give clients who need to contact a particular group. Be ready to urge a client to visit another chapter of the group if he or she does not like the first one attended. Groups have personalities that vary from one location to another.

*Follow the law.* In my state and many others, anyone who discovers that a child under a certain age has been the victim of physical or sexual abuse must by law report the fact to the Department of Children and Family Services. Let's suppose that a man comes to you, tearfully confessing that he has been inappropriately fondling his teenage daughter, and that she has threatened to tell Mom. He says he will stop, and he comes to you to show good faith about his intentions. But he doesn't want anyone else to know, because it will create an unnecessary scandal and perhaps break up his marriage.

Do not conspire with the man to keep this hushed up. Tell him that the law requires the matter to be reported—and that either he makes the phone call in your presence, or you will immediately do so yourself. The man's case will go better for him with the law, and probably in the eyes of his wife and daughter, if he takes responsibility to report himself and arrange to get any therapy necessary to modify his own behavior and heal his family's traumas.

## Playing Devil's Advocate

Remember my reference to how Mary Poppins got two rebellious children to go to sleep when they had refused? She wisely agreed with them in words: "Stay awake; don't sleep and dream." But she put these words into a lullaby that fostered the sleep that the kids were ready for.

Paradoxical techniques have become popular in recent years, particularly in the field of family therapy and/or to circumvent clients' resistances to doing things that will benefit them. Note, however, that the technique calls for more subtlety than just "getting people to do something by telling them to do the opposite." For instance, never tell people to commit suicide in order to keep them alive. Whenever you use reverse psychology, you must be willing for the client to *either* follow or defy your paradoxical prescriptions.

Earlier in this book I demonstrated how to budge people off the fence when they present you with equally strong arguments on both sides of a decision. Also, with Christians who stubbornly insist, for example, that they can't believe God loves them, I take the devil's-advocate position and argue for the case that I want them to abandon. I agree that God probably does *not* love them, adding further evidence to support a picture of God as cruel and untrustworthy. I might cite a recent disaster in the news, such as a tornado, and insist that if God had as much love in his entire being as I have in my little finger, he would have prevented it. This kind of outrageous argument often blasts clients into defending God's character.

Some of our bodily reactions actually work paradoxically. For example, if you try to keep your hands from sweating or your knees from knocking in an important social setting that you fear, they will sweat and knock all the more. You might calm them down by deliberately trying to make them sweat and knock. One way to take control of spontaneous behaviors that annoy you is to consciously do them more intensely. When you do that, you establish yourself as the controller of how much you do the actions. You can directly teach this principle to clients annoyed by their own uncontrolled mannerisms and seeking a first-aid technique to achieve control.

One particular paradoxical technique should be a routine part of your counseling tools. When clients get very enthusiastic or optimistic about some changes they begin to make, tell them to slow down. Predict setbacks. Restrain eagerness. Remind people that good results often seem apparent just from novelty effects and that only a few really dependable methods of solving problems stand the test of time.

This restraint-of-change technique keeps people from swinging like pendulums, from extreme enthusiasm to despondency when their initial high hopes do not continue to come to pass consistently. It also can marshal the best side of stubbornness, goading them to prove to you that the changes they have made are among the rare minority that do stand the test of time.

## Ricocheting

If I see two or more clients together, such as in marital therapy, I hold conversations with each about the other as a way to deliver interpretations indirectly to that other. I do this most often when the one we talk about is there as a visitor, not a customer. The therapy on non-customers is done by ricocheting insights about them off their partners.

For example, a wife complains that her husband is "too quick" with her sexually. Instead of my asking him what's going on with him, I ask *her* to guess, in his presence, what her husband might be feeling when he's being too quick. She seldom can answer, so I suggest that he probably fears looking inadequate. Or that maybe he might regard himself as a weakling instead of a real man if he took time to tenderly pleasure his wife. Perhaps long ago as a kid it was essential for him to act tough in order to be somebody and to avoid the shriveling belittlement of being called a sissy.

After I hold this discussion with the wife, she typically becomes much softer and more pensive about her husband. At that point I turn to the husband and ask him if there was anything he disagreed with in the guesses I made about him. Almost always he says *no,* largely because wording my question that way spares him from having to describe his childhood. By this procedure the wife's attitude toward the husband moves from displeasure and disapproval into a compassionate readiness to help her husband learn how to pleasure her. She becomes ready to reassure him that he is doing okay and that the more time he takes with her, the more manly he is in her eyes. She comes to see this approach as potentially more fruitful than the badgering complaints or sullen, quiet resentment that she displayed because of his inadequate lovemaking.

## Creating Researchers

When people shrink from the difficulty of some task that faces them, they need a different way to view it. A military man has to send soldiers to their death in battle. A woman faces breast surgery. An administrator has to fire a best friend for incompetence. A Christian missionary hesitates to return from furlough to work among unresponsive adherents to a false religion. These persons have all resolved to take the right actions, but they may fail to do so, out of discouragement.

You can help such clients by recommending an experimental attitude. Suggest that they enter their ordeals like news reporters, with their eyes wide open as if to notice every detail, so that they could later write a book about it to younger persons facing similar ordeals. Point out that they stand on the brink of earning veteran status. Since they are going to do it anyway, they might as well glean as much experience about it as possible and thereby pave the way for others. You may even dub them with the honorable title of "Pioneer in the Valley of the Shadow."

This perspective can liberate sufferers in three ways:

1. While suffering, they *also* perform a service for others.

2. By observing, they detach themselves from a central focus on their pain. The curious question—"What is this like?"—has a more soothing effect than the alarming thought, "I'm sure I can't stand this."

3. Also by observing, they stand enough outside the experience to lessen their human inclination to worship themselves for their martyrdom. After all, the term *self-pity* is a shortened form of *self-piety*.

Recently psychotherapy has seen a shift in emphasis from sickness to health. The former focus on *problems* has transferred to *solutions* (the current buzz word). This emphasis is typified in two books (de Shazer, 1985; O'Hanlon and Weiner-Davis, 1989) which enhance the material found on page 154 (Tilting Toward Health).

# 9

# A Verbatim Example

This chapter presents a nearly hour-long dialogue between a counselor (CO) and a client (CL). It is a totally hypothetical conversation, created simply to demonstrate the tactics presented in this book. The counselor's reasoning in choosing one option over another is printed in italics at various significant points in the interview.

If you happen to be a pastoral counselor who has occasion to set appointments in an office setting for as long as an hour, you may find yourself interested in almost all of this dialogue. But if you have less formal and shorter counseling opportunities, you may wish to concentrate on certain parts that you think would make the greatest immediate and enduring impact on your typical clients.

This illustration features a married Christian woman in her mid-thirties who called the counselor (a man) earlier this day, urgently insisting that he listen to her immediately. He quickly established some of the control that both he and she needed him to assert. Although the counselor agreed that the woman's urgent concerns merited prompt attention, he set a time workable for *him* a few hours later and in a place of *his* choosing. By these simple starting ground rules, he let the client know that she could rely on him not to let her problems overwhelm *him* as they had her. His initial goals for the upcoming session are (1) to calm her hysteria; and (2) to build into her some safeguards against recurrences of similar crises.

CO: What do you want my help with? [*Orients the conversation toward a purpose, rather than just opening the floor for the client to deliver a report of whatever she can think of to say.*]

CL: Everything's going wrong. I'm a nervous wreck. I have *no* self-esteem. My husband is no help; he says it's all in my head.

175

I'm not sure I even want to be married to him any more. I'm totally out of fellowship with God. I just can't go on like this.

CO: So, to say you are feeling overloaded is putting it mildly. [*Briefly sympathizes, to merge traffic with her.*]

CL: It sure is! I'm ready to crack. In fact, I think I might be having a nervous breakdown. Am I?

CO: Not at all. You simply have a lot to deal with at once, and we need to take things one at a time. So tell me this: did you feel *this* bad at this time yesterday? [*Briefly reassures, then begins to narrow the focus of client's complaints.*]

CL: No, not this bad. But I've always had low self-esteem, and I'm just at the end of my rope now. I don't think I can stand another minute. Oh, what am I going to do? Everything's—

CO: So, did you wake up feeling this bad first thing this morning? [*Interrupts client's escalation of hysterical panic. Sidesteps the self-esteem issue as an unworkable red herring. Returns to narrowing the problem focus.*]

CL: No, not this bad, just the usual misery I've been feeling for . . . I don't know how long. Is this normal? I mean, does God want me to go on suffering like this? I can't take it. I just—

CO: So, you didn't feel this bad when you woke up, but you did by about ten-thirty, when you called me. What happened in between those times? [*Interrupts escalation again and again refocuses on the quest for the precise conditions that spawned the client's crisis. Ignores the philosophical and theological questions at this time as less valuable to talk about than the still-unknown spark that lit her emotional conflagration.*]

CL: My whole world went to pieces, that's all!

CO: Specifically what went wrong? [*Pursues the search for a precise problem statement.*]

CL: Oh, just everything. My daughter dawdled and was late for the school bus, so I had to drive her, and we fought all the way. I don't know, just everything fell apart.

CO: When was the last time you and your daughter fought over her dawdling? [*Recognizes that the specific conflict the client mentioned probably represents the root of her present distress more than the global "everything" she emphasizes. Asking,*

*"When was the last time . . ." also elicits more specific informa-*
*tion than such similar questions as: "How often do you and*
*your daughter fight?" Getting specific requires clients to think,*
*which is perhaps the best first aid for runaway emotions.]*

CL: That's just the point. It used to be a problem last year, but
she's been real good about it all this year so far until today.
Now we're back to Square One. The problem wasn't really
solved. I'm a failure as a mother. I never do anything right.

CO: Was your daughter's dawdling a problem *all* last year, right
up through the very last day? [*Looks for exceptions and the
previous solution that worked for a while. Ignores the tempting
sidetracks of the client's exaggerated self-blame statements.*]

CL: No, she did better for about the last week of last year, and
then she started off okay this year. So I thought we had the
problem licked, but now I see I was mistaken and we haven't
really accomplished anything.

CO: What made her do better the last week of last year? [*Looks
for successful past solutions to transfer to the present problem.*]

CL: Well, my husband just laid the law down, saying that it was
her responsibility to get herself to the bus on time, and if she
didn't make it, we wouldn't drive her; she'd have to walk.

CO: Did she test that law before today? [*Embeds the reframe
word "test" within the question, as an indirect explanation of
what the daughter is now doing.*]

CL: No, I guess she thought we meant it, so she didn't risk it.

CO: Until today. [*Increases directness of the interpretation of the
girl's behavior as testing Mom's resolve to follow through with
enforcing the rule.*]

CL: Until today? You mean you think she's testing me to see if I
will make her walk to school if she misses the bus?

CO: Exactly! And what did she learn from her little experiment?
[*Takes a firm, direct position, knowing it brings more settling
structure into an emotionally volatile situation than do tentative answers like, "Well, what do you think?" or "I'm not sure,
but it's a possibility." Then invites the client to think, using
lighthearted wording that normalizes the daughter's misbehavior and neutralizes some of the mother's overreaction.*]

CL: You're saying I shouldn't have driven her.

CO: What do you think would have happened if you had simply followed through with the stated consequences and had refused to drive your daughter to school when she dawdled and missed the bus? [*Invites the client to think the unthinkable by carefully spelling out the appropriate action for her to take to resolve her problem.*]

CL: I could never do that. I wouldn't have the heart.

CO: What do you think would happen if you did? [*Simply repeats the salient question that the client has not yet addressed.*]

CL: My daughter would have a fit. I would never hear the end of it. She would make me feel like a bad mother.

CO: Would she stay home from school? [*Pursues the question of specifically what will happen.*]

CL: Oh, no. She loves school.

CO: So, if you don't drive your daughter to school when she misses the bus, she *will* walk, right? She has the motivation to get herself there one way or another? [*Explicitly summarizes the answer that the client has given but not considered.*]

CL: Hmm, well, yes, I suppose that's true. Hmm.

CO: Does it matter to her *how* she gets herself to school? I mean is it just as acceptable to her to walk as to ride the bus? [*Challenges client's unstated logic.*]

CL: Oh, horrors, no! She would hate having to walk. Not even mainly the effort of it, but the embarrassment would *kill* her.

CO: So, if you refuse to drive her when she dawdles and misses the bus, and you convince her that you are *not* going to drive her, no matter how she tests and manipulates you, how many mornings will she probably miss the bus? [*Again embeds the prescribed action within a question that calls for the client to think the unthinkable.*]

CL: I'm sure she would not miss more than once. She would *hate* having to walk.

CO: And how long will she continue to throw a tantrum at you for not driving her, as she hurries to get herself to her bus on time? [*Makes a strategic shift in wording from speculative "would" to future certainty "will." Embeds this implied positive prophecy within a question about the unthinkable.*]

CL: Hmm—I see what you're getting at. As soon as she makes up her mind to get herself to the school bus, she has no reason to fight with me. She won't waste the time and effort.

CO: Does that sound to you like a desirable enough outcome that you are willing to invest in it by tolerating the one uncomfortable day on which she *does* apply her tantrum tactics to you? [*Reframes the client's heretofore unthinkable toleration as an "investment." Asks for a decision that can settle the issue for the client before the stressful showdown with her daughter.*]

CL: Well, when you put it that way—hmm—you know, I never thought of it that way before, but since it would help my daughter to develop a good habit, it really would be an investment in her future. That makes sense to me. I'll do it!

CO: How about your husband—will he be proud of you? Or will he call you a cruel monster? How will you feel when *you* support what was originally *his* rule? [*Shifts to another of the problems the client originally mentioned—marital discord. Does so in a way likely to launch the topic on a positive note.*]

CL: Now there's a heavy topic. My husband and I have not been seeing eye to eye for a long time. In fact we hardly see each other at all since he got his new promotion on the job. Work is all he thinks about any more.

CO: If a miracle suddenly happened and the problems in your marriage were instantly solved, but no one told you about it, what would be the first signs that would let you know, "Something is different!"? [*Starts the client thinking about a positive future, so as to set some goals for focus in counseling. Also embeds within the question the statement "Something is different" as if it is already a part of the client's own thinking.*]

CL: Well, my husband would be spending more time at home. We would do things together as a family and as a couple, just he and I. We wouldn't fight as much. Maybe we would visit some of the friends we left behind when we moved from New Jersey.

CO: What kind of things have you and your husband enjoyed doing together in the past, just the two of you? [*Transfers past solutions to the present problem in the area that will probably benefit the whole family the most at this time: sweetening the marriage.*]

CL: Back in New Jersey we used to have this little out-of-the-way Japanese restaurant where we'd go. I mean, this was the real thing—shoes off, kimono on—the whole nine yards. It was very romantic. It reminded us of when we were first married and lived in Japan, where he was in the service.

CO: So, do you think he'd go for it if you did a little research and made a reservation for two at a similar Japanese restaurant around here—and surprised him? [*Proposes direct transfer of a former solution to solve a new problem.*]

CL: Wow! Hey, I think he would. In fact, his birthday is coming up. I think that would be just the time.

CO: You really miss New Jersey, don't you? [*Raises new problem topic, paving the way for client's grieving.*]

CL: I sure do. Leaving there was like tearing part of my insides out.

CO: An idea comes to me. You know how they say a picture is worth a thousand words? I'd like you to picture New Jersey, I mean all that it meant to you, as a kind of collage of people's faces, places, sights and sounds and smells—your house, the neighborhood, your church—as if they're all kind of joined together in a tearful send-off to you. Can you see that? [*Uses imagery to facilitate the emotional work of letting go her old attachment.*]

CL: I sure can. There's Mildred and Freddie. I even see our old dog, Bowser, who died a month before we left. Oh, this breaks my heart.

CO: You bet it does. And what do you feel like saying to them all? [*Fosters grieving by agreeing and asking for words that express it.*]

CL: I miss you guys—oh, how I miss you guys. You're all so special to me. I don't have anyone else like you now. I want to be back there with you.

CO: Now add the words, "But I'm here now and you're there, and we both have to make the best of it." [*Urges more actual statements of the decisions involved in mourning.*]

CL: Yeah, that's true. "I'm here and you're there and we both just have to accept it." I know I'm not going to move back.

CO: Now I want you to see an amazing thing happen in this

picture in your mind's eye. And tell me if this makes sense to you. See each one of those pictures in the collage take the form of a building block, a living stone, as the Bible says. Then Jesus, as the Master Builder, takes each one and lovingly arranges them together to form a foundation under a house that represents your life. In other words, your memories go with you, so that you always have New Jersey with you as part of the excellent foundation of the rest of your life. [*Uses imagery to reframe past attachments not as "lost" but as "built in."*]

CL: Oh, that's lovely. Yes, that does make sense to me.

CO: Now tell me more about what's going on with your husband. What's all of this moving and job pressure doing to *him*? [*Returns to another aspect of the marital issue, aiming to arouse compassion in the client toward her mate.*]

CL: I don't know for sure. We don't see much of him lately.

CO: Well, do you suppose he's real thrilled to get away from you and the kids? Is his job a gigantic relief from the unbearable responsibilities of family life? [*Plays mild devil's advocate to prompt client to recognize husband's caring.*]

CL: No, I'm sure he misses us. He really is a good father and a fairly decent husband. It's just that he's been so emotionally distant lately.

CO: To put that another way, could you say that giving devoted attention to handling his job responsibilities is really costing him something—probably a lot of loneliness? [*Reframes husband's "aloofness" as painful, rather than gratifying to him.*]

CL: You know, it must.

CO: Let's go a step further with the picture idea. If you could *see* your husband's loneliness symbolized somehow, what might it look like? A weight on his shoulders, an icy vise gripping his chest—what? [*Asks for imagery to arouse client's emotions to go with her intellectual insight about husband's feelings.*]

CL: I see it as a big hole inside him, like in his heart, or maybe his stomach—like hunger.

CO: What does that picture make you feel like *doing*? [*Asks a key question to connect head and heart inclinations into a unity that motivates client to action.*]

CL: It makes me want to feed him. This may sound silly, but I nursed each of my babies and loved it. I mean I really felt like I was *giving* them something of *me*. And in the picture, I want to do that for my husband. I want to feed him.

CO: So, what does that translate into in real life? What can you do that will feed your husband's lonely insides this week? [*Asks for action goals transferred from the symbolism in the imagery.*]

CL: Probably let him know I appreciate him. I don't think he's been getting much appreciation lately, either at home or at work.

CO: Next time you and I talk, will you let me know how you did that? [*Asks for accountability to motivate the client to follow through with her good intentions.*

CL: Sure. It's a deal.

CO: Now, you mentioned that you have felt out of fellowship with God lately. How will you know when you are in good, close fellowship with him? [*Returns to another of the client's original problems. Asks for criteria of solution.*]

CL: I guess when I don't feel any more as if he let me down. You see, I have been mad at God for not sparing my mother's life. She got congestive heart failure and the doctor told her she would have to lose eighty pounds and stop smoking. She wouldn't do it just because the doctor ordered it, and so I prayed that God would make her *want* to. I mean I've heard of drug addicts for whom God just took away their desire for narcotics. Why couldn't he have done that for my mother? I know God is a miracle-working God, and so when my mother first learned that she had this heart condition, I started praying that God would cure her by a miracle. I've heard and read stories where he did it for others. I prayed long and hard, so why did God not hear me?

CO: Could you try this statement on for size? It may sound kind of screwy, but I just had a flash of an idea. Could you see how this fits: "I am mad at God for not obeying me"? [*Challenges logic, cushioning it with disclaimers. Resists the temptation to comment on the need for the mother to do her part to be cured.*]

CL: "I *am* mad at God for not obeying me!" That really says it.

CO: Sure, because you worked hard, you prayed hard for your

mom's cure. You paid your dues, so you felt as if God *owed* you the miracle you wanted. [*Takes mild devil's advocate position, agreeing with client's perspective, then exaggerating it with an indirect logical challenge.*]

CL: Well, I know that God can't *force* people to do what's best for them, but he's God. He runs this universe, so I just expected him to—

CO: Could you say, "I wanted God to override my mother's free will"? [*Challenges logic again.*]

CL: Yes, I did. That's true.

CO: And *you* would have, if you were God. [*Maintains the momentum of a logical-challenge series, building up to one that will sharply arrest client's attention.*]

CL: Oh, you bet.

CO: Could you say, "I would disregard my mother's freedom of choice"? [*Slightly escalates logical challenge.*]

CL: "I would disregard my mother's freedom of choice." Yeah.

CO: Next statement: "That's how little I respected her." [*Challenges logic, highlighting the self-oriented aspect of client's anger at God, which crowds out her sadness about Mom and keeps her from grieving.*]

CL: Oh—oh—[More tears.]

CO: Do you follow what I'm saying? [*Follows up to deepen impact of logical challenge.*]

CL: Yeah.

CO: It's like you wanted to be the parent, with absolute power to boss and control your mom. [*Directly interprets her motives, because she seems open to it.*]

CL: Well, Mom was so opinionated, so stubborn—

CO: Now say this: "I would not permit my mother to be the kind of woman she wanted to be." [*Challenges logic again.*]

CL: "I would not permit my mom to be the kind of woman she wanted to be."

CO: True or false? [*Asks for response to logical challenge.*]

CL: True.

CO: Next statement: "I thought I had the power to keep her from being what she shouldn't be." [*Continues logical-challenge sequence.*]

CL: Well, Jesus has the power.

CO: What about *you*? [*Refocuses on the question at hand.*]

CL: You mean I was trying to act like God, lording it over Mom?

CO: Uh huh. No wonder you felt so frustrated. You must have been exhausted! [*Empathizes with client's probable emotions.*]

CL: I was so unhappy. I just wanted Mom to have what she always deserved—to see her grandchildren grow up and everything.

CO: So, could I say that you're in a big disagreement with God about how the universe ought to run? [*Delivers modified logical challenge.*]

CL: How?

CO: He allows people to make dumb choices and bear the natural consequences of them, reaping what they sow, and you don't like that policy. [*Mixes modified logical challenge with plain teaching to the now open-minded client.*]

CL: I just felt that he could intervene in some way, you know?

CO: In other words, "God *has* to do what he's *able* to do if I want him to." [*Challenges logic.*]

CL: Gosh, when you say it that way—you know, I sound like a spoiled brat stamping her angry little feet.

CO: Ah, so. I read about you in a book Jim Dobson wrote. [*Supports her confessional insight and normalizes it with playfulness.*]

CL: Which one? *The Strong-Willed Child?* It's funny. My boss told me I'm strong-willed. It kind of scares me, but lately I just want to be left alone.

CO: I hope this doesn't sound insulting. I don't know if you would use this word, but might you refer to this being left alone as a form of pouting? [*Cushions, then reframes negatively to make client's own behavior less acceptable to her.*]

CL: Hmm, probably—yes.

CO: It's a strong-willed child's way of punishing the world. [*Teaches.*]

CL: Yeah! If you don't let me have my way, I'll pick up my marbles and go home!

CO: You know, we've just about run out of time today. Before we finish up, I want to check with you on a couple of other questions. First of all, when people contact me for counseling, they often have been feeling so desperate that they have not even wanted to go on living. Have you had any such feelings lately? [*Makes transition to conclusion and approaches no-suicide decision.*]

CL: I sure have.

CO: Did you have any thoughts of harming yourself? [*Directly asks about suicidal intent.*]

CL: Yes.

CO: What did you think you might do? [*Explores seriousness of intent.*]

CL: I was just going to take an overdose, go to sleep and never wake up.

CO: How did you decide not to? [*Further explores seriousness of suicidal intent, but words the question this way to emphasize suicide as a decision within the client's power, not an impulse that overtakes her, and also to highlight the fact that the client has already opted for life when* feeling *suicidal.*]

CL: I just couldn't put my kids through such a thing.

CO: Will you make a firm decision right now, with me as witness, that you are never going to take your own life, no matter what? [*Directly asks for no-suicide decision.*]

CL: I suppose I should.

CO: You sound a little unsure. Let me offer you the words to say. Then you say them after me and see if they really express your decision: "I will never take my own life, either accidentally or on purpose, no matter what." [*Promotes deliberate, memorable decision.*]

CL: "I will never kill myself, no matter how bad I feel, either—" What was the other part?

CO: "Either accidentally or on purpose." Do you know what that means? [*Checks for thorough understanding.*]

CL: I'm not sure.

CO: That you're not going to be so careless that a so-called accident kills you. [*Closes all loopholes, meanwhile delivering a positive prophecy.*]

CL: Okay, I see what you mean. No, I won't do that.

CO: Better say the whole thing. [*Clarifies client's uncertain meaning by refocusing to the question at hand.*]

CL: "I will never kill myself, no matter what happens, either deliberately or by being careless." Did I say it right?

CO: That's fine. Now, do those words represent *your* decision? [*Asks for commitment.*]

CL: Yes.

CO: And if you ever *feel* like killing yourself, what will you do instead? [*Closes loopholes to reduce impulsiveness.*]

CL: I'll call someone before I do anything foolish.

CO: That's a good idea. Now, are there any other foolish actions that you need to rule out in a similar way? Like, have you been thinking lately of harming someone else, or quitting a job, or running away, or going crazy, or filing for divorce? [*Searches for any other loopholes to close.*]

CL: I thought of running away—how nice it would be to just leave all my pressures.

CO: Will you rule that out, too? [*Builds on momentum of no-suicide decision by directly asking for another decision against impulsive, harmful action.*]

CL: Yes. I won't run away.

CO: Anything else we should be sure to talk about today, something that can't wait until the next time we meet? [*Moves to closure. Clears up loose ends. Reassures client that they can meet again.*]

CL: No, I'm feeling a lot better now than when I called you.

CO: Fine. Then what I'd like to do before we wind up for today is to excuse myself for a few minutes and go into another room to think over what we've talked about and come up with some recommendations. [*Initiates think break, arousing client's curiosity about conclusions and recommendations.*]

CL: Okay. Shall I just wait here?

CO: Yes, I'll be right back. [*By simple, direct manner gives client his vote of confidence that she can manage herself just fine. No fear-inducing questions like, "Are you going to be okay if I leave you alone for a few minutes?"*]

CO: *Takes five-minute think break, writing down five compliments that summarize high points of the session and also noting two prescriptions to deliver.*]

CO: [*upon returning*] Well, I enjoyed that chance to review what we covered in our time today. I was particularly impressed at how deeply you care about harmony between people. You wanted it between you and your daughter, you and your husband, your mom and Jesus, and yourself and God. It's a strong feature in your makeup—a passion for harmony. [*Launches compliments by positively reframing the anguish that prompted client's crisis.*]

Another strong trait that really comes through as you talk is your loyalty. You expressed it toward New Jersey and toward Mom. [*Continues, not letting client break the flow of the compliment list and thus dull its impact. Accepting and admiring her devotion to New Jersey lessens her need to continue living back there mentally.*]

And what a romantic flair you showed as you talked about the Japanese restaurant! That was inspiring! [*Reinforces client's intention to rekindle sparks of affection in her marriage.*]

I was also struck by your keen ability to put yourself in another person's shoes, like your husband's, as we talked about how *he's* feeling lately. You could quickly sense his loneliness, and you let compassion mellow within you into the kind of perfect love that casts out fear, certainly yours, and maybe also his. [*Reminds client of her new view of her husband as "lonely" rather than "uncaring." Frames feedback in scriptural terms that appeal to this devout lady.*]

Furthermore, I was moved by your love for life. It came through in your zesty playfulness throughout our conversation, in the intensity with which you are able to feel emotion, and in the fact that you *kept* yourself alive even before your no-suicide decision here today. [*Cites client's humorous bent as a strength, which she may not have thought of before. Reframes her hysteria as a lively capability, making her more consciously aware*]

*of it, without defensiveness, which would interfere with her re-*
*examining it. Confirms her decision not to kill herself.]*

Now, there's something I'd like you to do between now and the
next time we meet. We have focused mostly today on things
that have been going *wrong* in your life recently. As you put it,
*everything* seemed like it was going wrong. But I'd like you to
take an inventory of your life, your family, your circumstances,
and notice what is going on that you want to continue to have
go as it is. Is that clear? [*Delivers the Inventory Task prescrip-*
*tion, and in the process mildly caricatures the hysterical escala-*
*tion with which the client called earlier in the day, so that she*
*cannot do it as automatically in the future.*]

CL: You want me to list what's going right.

CO: That's right. And also there was one other thing you said
you will tell me next time. Remember? [*Leads up to second*
*prescription.*]

CL: No, what do you mean?

CO: Finding that little out-of-the-way romantic rendezvous?
[*Playfully jogs client's memory, thus diminishing any obli-*
*gatory flavor about the assignment.*]

CL: Oh, yeah. I'm going to arrange a birthday celebration for my
husband at some Japanese restaurant.

CO: Right! And I have another thought, too. The reason I asked
your permission to run a tape recorder was so that you could
have the tape to take home with you and listen to a playback.
Do you have access to a cassette player? [*Adds a third home-*
*work assignment.*]

CL: Sure, there's one in the car, and I can borrow one from the
kids.

CO: Fine. I'll give you the tape. You can just bring it back next
time, and I will erase it and re-use it. Some people even listen
to their tapes a couple of times and make notes on them that
they bring here to discuss with me. Incidentally, do you think
your husband might be interested in listening to the tape?
Does he know you were planning to talk to a counselor? [*Indi-*
*rectly suggests ways client can get the most out of the tape. Also*
*sets the stage for counseling the husband by ricochet.*]

CL: No, he doesn't know I'm here. That's okay, though, I'll tell him I came. But I don't know if I want him to hear the tape. I don't even know if *I* want to hear it. I must have sounded like some kind of a weirdo. Did I? Do you think I'm crazy?

CO: Hang on a minute. Thinking of your husband listening to the tape—was there anything we discussed here that you would *not* have said with him present? [*Refocuses on the question at hand.*]

CL: Hmm—no, not really. I think it would be okay.

CO: Well, I tell you what. Take the tape and listen to it yourself. Then, if your husband expresses interest in hearing it, you have my permission to let him. [*Gently reassigns tape-listening to the client, who has expressed reluctance, and does it within the larger context of allowing the husband to hear it.*]

CL: Okay.

CO: How's this same time for you again next Tuesday? [*Sets follow-up appointment.*]

CL: That's fine.

CO: I'll see you then. [*Announces the end of the session.*]

CL: [*at the doorknob*] Is there any hope for me? Am I gonna be all right?

CO: You amaze me! [*Uses therapeutic astonishment to sidestep client's bid for additional reassurance that would do more to erode her confidence than to build it.*]

CL: Why?

CO: You actually asked *my* opinion about your future instead of announcing your own! [*Puts responsibility back on client to take courage, instead of always viewing herself as needing to get it from someone else.*]

CL: Well, you're the expert.

CO: Now I'm even *more* amazed! [*Again uses therapeutic astonishment to sidestep client's dependency ploy.*]

CL: Why?

CO: Because you're *still* doing it! [*Continues confrontation of passivity.*]

CL: Well, I just thought—Oh, what's the use? You'll just tell me I'm doing it again. I might as well just go. This *has* been helpful. Thank you. I'll see you next week.

CO: Thank *you!* And goodbye! [*Closes decisively on a friendly note.*]

# References

Berne, E. (1964). *Games people play.* New York: Grove Press.

Burns, D. (1980). *Feeling good.* New York: Morrow.

de Shazer, S. (1985). *Keys to solution in brief therapy.* New York: Norton.

Drummond, H. (1959). *The greatest thing in the world.* London: Hodder and Stoughton.

Frankl, V. E. (1963). *Man's search for meaning.* New York: Pocket Books.

Gibson, D. L. (1987). *The strong-willed adult.* Grand Rapids, Mich.: Baker.

Gordon, T. (1970). *Parent effectiveness training.* New York: Wyden.

Hunt, D., and McMahon, T. A. (1985). *The seduction of Christianity.* Eugene, Oreg.: Harvest House.

James, W. (1890). *The principles of psychology,* Vols. 1 and 2. New York: Holt.

Lloyd-Jones, D. M. (1965). *Spiritual depression.* Grand Rapids, Mich.: Eerdmans.

Masterson, J. F. (1976). *Psychotherapy of the borderline adult: a developmental approach.* New York: Brunner/Mazel.

Munger, R. B. (1986). "My heart—Christ's home" (revised edition). Downers Grove, Ill.: InterVarsity.

O'Hanlon, W. H., and Weiner-Davis, M. (1989). *In search of solutions.* New York: Norton.

Reid, T. F.; Virkler, M.; Laine, J. A.; and Langstaff, A. (1986). *Seduction? A biblical response.* New Wilmington, Penn.: Son-Rise Publ.

Seamands, D. (1985). *Healing of memories.* Wheaton, Ill.: Victor.

Weiner-Davis, M. (1988). *Personal communication.* New York: Norton.

## DATE DUE